The story of Joseph is a great [example of] God's providence. But a sym[phony is brought to] life by a skilled expert who und[erstands] all the nuances of the music. Enter Liam Golig[her and we] know the music is in safe hands. In his hands the Joseph Symphony intrigues, delights, and captivates our hearts for God and his ways and fills us with admiration for his wise providence. Here is a book to put melody into the way we live the Christian life.

Sinclair B Ferguson
The First Presbyterian Church
Columbia, USA

Here's an excellent, insightful and contemporary introduction to an ancient 'soap opera': a family's fortunes that have turned the course of history, by the astonishing grace and providence of God, through their greatest relative, Jesus the Saviour of the world. Highly recommended!

Dr Steve Brady, Principal
Moorlands College
Christchurch, UK

Joseph

The Hidden Hand of God

Liam Goligher

CHRISTIAN
FOCUS

Copyright © Liam Goligher 2008

ISBN 978-184550-368-0

Printed in 2008 by
Christian Focus Publications, Geanies House,
Fearn, Ross-shire, IV20 1TW, Scotland.

www.christianfocus.com

Cover design by moose77.com

Printed and bound in Denmark by Norhaven

Contents

1

Happy Families

Who doesn't know something about the story of Joseph? Even if it isn't familiar from school or Sunday school, most will have heard of the musical, *Joseph and the Amazing Technicolour Dreamcoat*. However, this isn't a story just for children or theatrical entertainment. The story of Joseph is one of the best-told stories of all time. It is the tale of a hero who overcomes all the odds, surviving childhood and the dangers of early adulthood to become a great man of his time. It has all the elements of a gripping story – conflict, envy, murderous intentions, sexual temptation, desperate circumstances, improbable coincidences and even supernatural interventions. If we think of the story of Joseph only in these terms, however, we shall miss its real significance, because it is actually part of a much bigger story, one which tells of God's dealings with humanity.

The story of Joseph, which appears in the first book of the Bible, marks a new departure in the unfolding drama of God's creation plan. The book of Genesis (meaning 'beginnings' or 'origins') opens with God's creation of a perfect world where people live in perfect harmony with Him.[1] Once people choose to go their own way instead of obeying God, things start to go wrong.[2] By the time of Joseph, God has started on His plan of redemption, choosing to create a people who would have a special relationship with Himself. It started with just one man, Abraham,[3] and progress was slow, because Abraham only had one son, Isaac, by his wife, and Isaac just had twins, Esau and Jacob.[4] God chose to develop his special family through Jacob's sons, and that's when the tribes of Israel (the new name which God gave to Jacob) were founded, because amazingly Jacob fathered twelve sons, one of whom was Joseph.

Family favourites
At one level the story of Joseph is the story of a dysfunctional family. That is not why the story is in the Bible, but the fact that it was that kind of family and that it has been recorded in Scripture, helps us to see not only the extent to which sin can spoil the closest of human relationships, but also how God can use even such dysfunctionality to further His purposes. Joseph was born into a complex family situation. There was one father, Jacob, but four mothers (two wives and two concubines), eleven sons and one daughter. When Joseph was still quite young, his mother Rachel had another son, Benjamin, but she died in childbirth. This is the background to the favouritism that Jacob showed to Joseph:

---

[1] Genesis 1 and 2
[2] Genesis 3 - 6 verse 7
[3] Genesis 12-22
[4] Genesis 25:19-26

Israel loved Joseph more than any of his other sons, because he was the son of his old age.[5]

He was also the firstborn of Rachel, the love of Jacob's life for whom he had had to work and wait seven years after being tricked into marrying her elder sister Leah. Rachel had fertility problems, whilst her sister produced with ease. By the time Rachel had Joseph, both women had vied for their husband's favour by getting their maids to act as surrogate mothers. The ensuing rivalries and tensions between the women and their children is not hard to understand. It must have been something of a nightmare for Jacob too![6]

You might have thought that Jacob would have learned from his own past. His father Isaac had favoured his brother Esau, and Rebekah, his mother, had preferred Jacob, resulting in a rivalry which ended in Jacob having to leave home under a cloud.[7] Yet now he loved some of his own children more than the others. Perhaps it was understandable that he should favour the children of his old age and his dearest wife, but there was no excuse for him to show it, and certainly not to accentuate it by marking out Joseph as he did when he gave Joseph his famous coat. Some people never learn!

There are people fortunate in having happy childhood memories of family life.

When I was young we loved to have company round to visit, especially family. Often, as the last person left, my mother would close the door, let out a feigned sigh, and

---

[5] Genesis 37:3
[6] Genesis 29 and 30
[7] Genesis 27 and 28

with a playful smile quote a line of an old hymn: 'Peace perfect peace, with loved ones far away!' She was only kidding of course, and my brother John and I knew that mum really loved having visitors, but we also knew she liked to have her house back to herself again. I smile as I think of her; she was great fun.

Other people don't have such happy memories of childhood, and the further they can get away from their 'loved ones' the better. As I write this, I have just been on the phone with an old friend whose childhood was miserable, whose father was always abusing his mother, and who was himself the object of abuse. To this day there is a legacy of bitterness and an inability to express affection, which is having a negative impact on the next generation. There is perhaps nothing more destructive to an individual than to be in a dysfunctional family. If your family life sometimes seems to be getting out of control or going terribly wrong, and you are finding that hard to bear, then this is a story with which you will empathise.

Clearly, Jacob's family was far from perfect, so we learn right at the beginning of the story that God can use imperfect people. In fact, the only material he ever has to work with is fallen, sinful and often deeply flawed, which means that He can work with someone just like you and me! So if your past is one you would rather forget, then let the story of Joseph give you hope that God can take the broken threads of your life and weave them into a beautiful tapestry that will give joy to others.

The big picture
Joseph's story, which begins in Genesis chapter 37, marks a new phase in God's plan. In the bigger picture of Scripture,

God is setting things up for a greater story, the redemption of His chosen people from Egypt. Before His people can be rescued from Egypt, however, they have first to get there, and this is where Joseph comes into the story.

Before looking at Joseph's life in detail, two principles of biblical interpretation need to be borne in mind. The first is that when reading these Old Testament stories, the biblical text must guide us in our interpretation. The bible is its own best interpreter. In fact this is how we should interpret all Scripture; it is clear and capable of interpreting itself. So we must be careful not to speculate beyond what is written.

The second principle is that we must not read the Old Testament (as many scholars do) as if the New Testament had not been written. We read it today as Christians, that is, as those who have the final revelation from God written in our New Testament. The Old Testament is still a Christian book, however; it is simply full of Christ. As someone has said, 'every story whispers his name' - and I would want to add that some Old Testament stories shout it out loud! So, after His resurrection, Jesus met His disciples and 'beginning with Moses and all the prophets, he interpreted to them in all the Scriptures the things concerning himself'.[8] Those 'Scriptures' were, of course, what we know today as the Old Testament.

Genesis 37:2 begins by saying, 'These are the generations of Jacob' The Hebrew word is '*toledoth*', which means 'generations'. Throughout Genesis it is used as a technical heading for each new section of the story. So, for example, in Genesis 2 it reads, 'These are the generations of the heavens and the earth when they were created.' Later we

---

[8] Luke 24:27

read about the 'generations of Adam ... of Noah ... of the sons of Noah ... of Shem ... of Terah (the father of Abraham) ... of Isaac ... of Esau ...' and now, 'of Jacob.' Up to this point in the book there were those who 'called on the name of the LORD.'[9] Among them was Abraham, the father of those who have faith. Now those who call upon God's name – the church of that age – are going to be called 'Israel', which was the new name given to Jacob by God Himself.[10] In fact even in the New Testament people who call upon the name of the Lord Jesus are called 'the Israel of God' by the apostle Paul.[11] This is the last time this heading (the generations of ...) is used in the whole Old Testament Scriptures, because the rest of the Old Testament is about the nation of Israel, the descendants of this individual. Joseph is used to set things up so that Israel might grow into a great nation in the safety of Egypt and later be redeemed by the mighty hand of God.[12]

The next time in the Bible that this expression ('*toledoth*') is used, it marks a new departure again. We find it used in Matthew chapter 1: 'The book of the genealogy of Jesus Christ, the son of David, the son of Abraham.' If Matthew had written in Hebrew, he would have used the same word as is used in Genesis ('*toledoth*'). What is Matthew telling us? He is saying that with the coming of Jesus into the world a new thing happened, something that continues the story, that picks up and fulfils promises made all the way back in Genesis. It is also worth noting that 'the generations of Jacob' begin and end with a Joseph. Joseph is the first

---

[9] Genesis 4:26
[10] Genesis 32:22-30
[11] Galatians 6:16
[12] Exodus chapters 1-14

name introduced after the 'generations of Jacob' appear in Genesis, and Joseph is the last name used in the genealogy of Jesus as detailed in Matthew.[13] Joseph, the legal father of Jesus, would be the last Joseph mentioned before the new *toledoth* of Jesus came in.

When God is invisible

That is the bigger picture of where the story of this seventeen-year-old boy Joseph is going. But none of that was known to him at this stage. In fact if you read the first chapter of his life, you will find that God's name doesn't appear at all.[14] Moses, who wrote this account, wanted his readers to ask the question, 'Why isn't God mentioned?' This is one of the author's teaching techniques. The absence of God's name is deliberate in order to provoke the question and make the reader or hearer think. Although God's name is not mentioned and His presence is not seen, he is nonetheless active in everything that takes place. The reality is that in your life and mine there are many days, and hours within days, when God's presence is not felt, when He seems miles away and when no reference either in thought or word is made to Him. To anyone looking on at the circumstances Joseph goes through, God does not appear to be involved. That's why secular writers can write about his life and miss the point of what is going on. That is also why our non-Christian friends can look at us and see no obvious sign that God is alive and at hand for us. Like them, we struggle to get up in the morning, we take colds and cancers, and we grow old and die. Circumstances over which we have no control often seem to determine the course of our lives; we make

---

[13] Genesis 37:2; Matthew 1:16

[14] Genesis 37

good and bad decisions, and God seems a million miles away. Very often the most 'spiritual' among us forget to consult Him and push on with our own agenda. That is what we find people doing in this story; that's the way the story is told because that's the way we are as human beings. Made by God, we ignore Him; provided for by Him, we forget to give thanks; loved by God, we don't return the compliment.

'Any dream will do'
Things were already in a pretty dreadful state in Jacob's family when our story begins. Joseph was seventeen and his brothers were grown men, but they were already annoyed by their father's obvious preference for Rachel's children. The 'coat of many colours' didn't help, of course. Its significance was that it indicated status as well as favour. It marked Joseph out as the management rather than the worker. It may even have implied to the brothers that their father might favour Joseph over them when it came to the question of inheritance. If there was anything guaranteed to make Joseph stand out as being a daddy's boy, that coat would do it.

> *Now Israel loved Joseph more than any other of his sons, because he was the son of his old age. And he made him a robe of many colours. But when his brothers saw that their father loved him more than all his brothers, they hated him and could not speak peacefully to him.[15]*

His brothers hated him for it. But there was more to their hatred than that.

The story begins by telling us that Joseph brought a 'bad report' of the boys to his father after doing a spot of

---

[15] Genesis 37:3-4

shepherding duty with his brothers. Was he asked to keep an eye on them? Did he spice up the report and make it sound worse than it was? Was he simply acting as a talebearer, a tattle-tale or a snitch? There is nothing in the text to suggest he may have been like this. Certainly his future behaviour gives no hint of his having a character flaw like that. One thing we do know from the previous chapters of Genesis is that it would not take much imagination to come up with something bad to say about them. Already these brothers had been up to some significant mischief. Reuben had slept with his father's concubine,[16] while Simeon and Levi had slaughtered virtually a whole tribe at Schechem because some of the men had disgraced their sister.[17] These men were constitutionally rough, reckless and dangerous. Very probably their father could not trust them to do what they were supposed to be doing for him. Yet it appears that he could trust Joseph, and later in this chapter we find him sending Joseph out to check that his sons were looking after the sheep properly.[18]

The really significant point of the early part of Joseph's story, however, has to do with his dreams. As was established earlier, God does not appear in this first chapter yet He is everywhere present. It is also true that He does not speak yet His voice is truly heard. That is because He had a witness:

Now Joseph had a dream... Then he dreamed another dream.[19]

God was communicating His word through Joseph's dreams.

---

[16] Genesis 35:22
[17] Genesis 34
[18] Genesis 37:12-14
[19] Genesis 37:5, 9

There are several different ways in Genesis in which God deals with His people. In chapters 1-11 He appears to people as a theophany, an appearance of God in the form of an angel or other mysterious figure. In chapters 12-35 He speaks to people in dreams and visions. Now, in chapters 36-50, He makes His will known without speaking directly to individuals. There is no prophetic word as such, yet He makes His purposes known second-hand, through a verbal witness. Joseph did not have the experiences his fathers had. He heard no voice speak to him; unlike Abraham, he had no mysterious visitors whose very presence left Abraham with a sense that God had visited him.[20] There was no great vision of a ladder stretching from earth to heaven,[21] nor a physical struggle with a heavenly being that lasted all night, such as his father Jacob had.[22] Joseph had to go through his life trusting God when God was both unseen and apparently silent. Even these dreams in chapter 37 contain no revelation of God or divine explanation to confirm their origin or their meaning. That they are of God is confirmed only with hindsight as they are fulfilled in the flow of history.

On the surface, Joseph's dreams are entirely secular and may even seem self-serving, but they are in fact, as we shall see, God's witness and sure word to the family. God never leaves Himself without a witness. He speaks to the world in every generation. The New Testament speaks about this witness:

In the past God spoke to our forefathers through the prophets at many times and in various ways.[23]

---

[20] Genesis 18
[21] Genesis 28:10-19
[22] Genesis 32:22ff
[23] Hebrews 1:1

In the culture of Joseph's time, dreams such as these were often thought to be a means of divine communication and prediction. Dreams were a demonstration of God's sovereignty, a declaration of the fact that He rules the world and the affairs of individuals. These dreams right at the beginning of the story are going to be fulfilled. They correctly outline the future as it is going to unfold, and they are a standing reminder that we all live our lives under the authority of the Word of God whether we are aware of it or not. One interesting fact to observe is that the dreams come in pairs to suggest certainty of fulfilment. It is this which probably drove Joseph to tell the family what he'd dreamt. Later on in Israel's history any message or word had to be established in the mouth of two witnesses. The two dreams act as two witnesses to Joseph's family of God's ultimate intention.

His first dream about the corn probably hints at the coming famine and the work that Joseph would do in Egypt. He was going to be responsible for providing corn for the whole Egyptian Empire and beyond. Certainly his brothers recognised right away what the dream suggested, because they said to him, 'Are you indeed to reign over us? Or are you indeed to rule over us?'[24]

The second dream has the sun, moon and eleven stars bowing down before him. It goes further than the first, and the message of not only his brothers but also his father and mother bowing down to him comes through clearly.

Why did Joseph tell them? Was he being brash, arrogant, or just foolish? All kinds of suggestions have been offered to explain his behaviour. Maybe it was simply that he felt bemused and quite excited at having two such dreams in

---

[24] Genesis 37:8

succession and felt the need to tell those who knew him best. I remember when I first went to Theological College in Ireland. On the first weekend there I was sent to preach in a country church. It was my first experience of preaching in Ireland. I was excited and rather nervous, but it went well and I was thrilled with the response of people. Next day, at lunch, I got into conversation with another first-year student. Perhaps I wanted to impress her; it may be I was feeling pleased with myself. I do know that I was quite 'high' after a good Sunday and that I needed to talk about it, but this girl went away thinking I was 'full of myself' and rather conceited. She wasn't impressed. I know how she felt, for she told me afterwards. We eventually married, and she has yet to give me her definitive view on what was going on that day! The point is that we don't know why Joseph told everyone about his dream, and the Bible gives us no reason to think ill of him, but we can be glad he did, because it meant that all of his family knew at the same time the story of these dreams which were to be fulfilled exactly as revealed. First his brothers bow down to him in Egypt[25]; then they bow again twice to honour him,[26] and then finally they throw themselves down at his feet fearing for their lives.[27] This perfect fulfilment of Joseph's dreams demonstrated to them many years later that they had heard the Word of God from their brother. There is a sense in which he had to tell because he was the voice of God to his family in that generation. He was unconscious of it and they were annoyed by it, indeed 'they hated him all the more',[28] but it was part of God's plan.

---

[25] Genesis 42:6
[26] Genesis 43:26, 28
[27] Genesis 50:18
[28] Genesis 37:8

This means that when they mocked Joseph, they were mocking the Word of God, and when they rejected Joseph, they were rejecting that same Word. The Bible says of Joseph that 'until what he said had come to pass, the word of the Lord tested him.'[29] When our Lord Jesus was on earth, He too was accused by His opponents of being brash, and even of blaspheming against God by the claims He was making. They despised Him and mocked him as a Nazarene and an uneducated man. They challenged the authority by which He spoke.

Today we are witnesses of a similar kind to Joseph. This is not a day of significant signs and wonders, though many wish it were. This is not the day of the Old Testament prophet nor of the New Testament apostle. There are no fresh words from God through specially appointed vessels. God is at work differently today, for He has given us a word for the world. No doubt it sounds brash on our lips. It proclaims our place in God's purposes; that we are 'children of God' and 'heirs of life'.[30] We are able to say from Scripture (the sure Word of God) that we have eternal life. And the world takes exception to what we say just as the brothers took exception to what Joseph said. After all, doesn't the Bible teach that believers will judge angels?[31] Isn't it arrogant to make such claims? Isn't it the height of nonsense to be so sure of our soul's salvation? Well, sometimes the way we express ourselves does make us sound arrogant. Perhaps there was a hint of pride in Joseph, though the text gives us no grounds for thinking that. But when we speak what God has said in His Word, we are simply telling the truth.

---

[29] Psalm 105:19
[30] Romans 8:16-17
[31] 1 Corinthians 6:3

It was this truth-telling that roused the hatred of his brothers, just as Jesus' declaration of truth roused the hatred of the authorities of His day. The brothers' rejection of Joseph is explained in terms of their rejection of the revelation given through him:

So they hated him all the more because of his dreams and for his words.[32]

You can see the emphasis on the 'words'. That is the Bible's own interpretation of their hostility. When they mocked Joseph's dreams, they were mocking the revelation of God.

Only one man wondered about what he had heard. 'His father kept the saying in mind.'[33] Even though he rebuked his son for being so brash, Jacob saw the truth in it: he recognised that God had spoken. He may not have seen how it could all be worked out, but he took it seriously. And God left Himself a witness. He had Joseph tell these dreams up front and share them with his family so that they would all remember, so that they would all be witnesses to the fact that before the events took place God had sent His witness. The experiences of their lives were not going to be the product of chance or the result of human decision, but were being guided and superintended by a God who works out everything in accordance with His purposes.[34]

---

[32] Genesis 37:8
[33] Genesis 37:11
[34] Romans 8:28

2
Sold for 20 Pieces of Silver!

We can never second-guess God. He has a habit of doing the counter-intuitive thing. Who would have thought that He would choose to work out His plan through a family like Jacob's, rife with favouritism, jealousy, immorality and vengeance? Yet that is precisely what he did. But before God could give this family a kingdom, he first had to rescue them from themselves. The next episode of this story takes events a step forward towards the outworking of that purpose.

Just an ordinary day
The action starts simply enough when Joseph is sent to check on his brothers.

> *And Israel said to Joseph, "Are not your brothers pasturing the flock at Shechem? Come, I will send you to them."*[1]

---

[1] Genesis 37:13

It seems incredible that Jacob could be so blind to the true feelings of his sons towards Joseph, but no doubt they were careful not to let their father see their simmering resentment – such are the ways of bullies in every generation! Even if Jacob didn't grasp the depths of his sons' hatred for Joseph, he could have been under no illusions about their general behaviour. By this stage it was in all probability at least two years since the atrocity perpetrated by the brothers at Shechem.[2] Given the brothers' past history, and having not heard from them for a while, it would be surprising if their father had not begun to wonder what they were up to. Perhaps this concern was so overwhelming to Jacob that he threw all natural caution to the wind. He just had to find out what they were doing.

Equally baffling is Joseph's ready response, 'Here I am.' He had already endured their scoffing reaction to his dreams and earned their disfavour for giving his father an unfavourable report of their activities. Now he was being sent on what would look like a spying trip. There might have been an eagerness to go, indicating a certain naïveté and an unawareness of their true feelings towards him, or perhaps he went with a heavy heart and some misgivings. Scripture does not tell us Joseph's state of mind. However he felt, what we do know is that Joseph was willing to obey his father.

Joseph takes the fifty-mile journey to Shechem on his own and ends up wandering around dangerously near the site of the massacre mentioned earlier. Grazing the flocks in that area might have looked provocative – could that have been one of Jacob's concerns? Did he just expect that they might be up to no good? Whatever the reason, it is there Joseph has his first encounter with God's 'providence'.

---

[2] Genesis 34

Providence is a word every Christian should know, for it refers to God's good government of our lives. We are not the victims of luck, fate or karma. Rather, God has mapped out our path from before time began. He is active in the circumstances, surprises and choices of our lives and is all the time leading us towards His purpose. As has been noted before, God's name is absent from the story at this point, yet He is everywhere present. He had been present in the dreams Joseph had and now He was present in the provision of a stranger to help him in the search for his brothers.

Intriguingly, the story of Joseph meeting a stranger is given considerable prominence in the text.

And a man found him wandering in the fields. And the man asked him, 'What are you seeking?' 'I'm seeking my brothers,' he said.[3]

From a secular world-view it was all a happy chance. If the man had not been there, and taken the initiative, Joseph might well have wandered aimlessly for a while, then given up; he might have gone back home and he would never have ended up in Egypt. But this is no mere chance encounter. God is at work setting the stage for His future purpose. It is also ironic that Joseph should be safer with a man from Shechem, their old family enemy, than he was to be in the hands of his own brothers. This idea of 'meeting a stranger' is to become a defining characteristic in the Bible of meeting with God.

What is striking is the ordinariness of it all. There are no supernatural elements, no hyper-spiritual occurrences. In fact, throughout Joseph's life there is little of supernatural

---

[3] Genesis 37:15

interest, on the surface at least. Like most of us, he had to live his life by the ordinary means of grace. His experience of God was cultivated by the ordinary and unspectacular. We are tempted sometimes to want to spiritualise the ordinary, to use 'words', to see 'pictures' or claim 'signs' that make life seem more exciting than it is. Joseph was lost and a stranger helped him. That is all the Bible says. There is no speculation in the text as to whom the stranger was, yet his intervention was crucial to the outworking of the story. It was surely the providence of God.

Our lives are made up of such ordinary things. Most of you reading this will never have anything 'supernatural' happen to you. Does that make you a failure? Does that mean you have a sub-standard Christian experience? Not at all, unless you are prepared to say that Joseph's experience too was sub-standard. It takes more faith and greater grace to live for God in days when his presence is invisible and His purposes are hidden from our eyes. We are meant to walk by faith and not by sight.

Into the pit
Having found out from the stranger where his brothers are, Joseph sets off to find them. It is as Joseph walks over the hill and his brothers see him from a distance that things begin to go wrong.

> *They saw him from afar, and before he came near to them they conspired against him to kill him.*

It is obvious they are still smouldering over the content of his dreams:

---

[4] Genesis 37:18 -20

'Here comes this dreamer, come now, let us kill him and throw him into one of the pits.'[4]

There were pits in that area which were bottle-shaped, narrow at the top and broadening out as they went down. They were hewn out of rock to retain water and would have been impossible to escape from. Once inside, a man would slowly starve to death.

These brothers were determined to frustrate the Word of God revealed through Joseph's dreams. Their hostility is presented as a threat to Joseph's divinely ordained role as the rescuer of many people:

'Then we'll see what comes of his dreams.'[5]

The brothers' hatred of Joseph was ultimately a hatred of God's revelation, because they were ignoring what they knew of God's will. How does this tie in with the concept of providence? Well, if Joseph had not been rejected by his brothers, he could never have become their saviour.

Resisting God's plan
There is nothing as painful as rejection. For some of us the only experience of being rejected amounts to not being picked for the school hockey or football team. Some will remember the daily dread of bullying at school. Others may have had the experience of applying for promotion, getting shortlisted and then being rejected at the end of the process. Other forms of rejection can go much deeper and hurt longer, as in cases such as a wife rejected in favour of a younger model, or a child rejected for not meeting high parental expectations.

[5] Genesis 37:20

I watched an episode of the TV drama *House* recently. House is a world-famous physician, noted for his diagnostic ability. He is confident to the point of arrogance and invariably right in his diagnoses. In this episode, his parents visit him, but he tries as hard as he can to avoid them. It becomes clear that the reason for this alienation is that his father views him as a cripple due to his limp, the result of an accident. This fact seems to blind the father to his son's real achievements and successes, and the rejection House feels hurts deeply. This begins to explain the way House verbally abuses the people with whom he works. It is as if by pushing them away, he is testing whether they truly care for him as he is, limp and all.

The factors that led to Joseph's rejection by his brothers are complex. That fancy coat was a constant irritation, a reminder of their father's favouritism, and that bad report still rankled. Imagine telling on your older brothers! Yet these things alone cannot explain the extreme hatred for the boy that had developed in these brothers, nor their murderous intention. Something deeper was going on, and the Bible helps us to understand precisely what it is.

Interestingly, nowhere does the narrative try to psychoanalyse their behaviour. It is more concerned with character than psychology. The text tells us that their hostility was based on their understanding of Joseph's dreams. They rightly interpreted his dreams to mean that he would 'reign' or 'rule' over them. Their hatred was based specifically on 'his dreams' and 'his words'.[6] Unlike the Pharaoh of Moses day, who failed to grasp the divine origin of the plagues,[7] the brothers understood the import of Joseph's dreams and they took them seriously. They could have dismissed him as being

---

[6] Genesis 37:8
[7] Exodus chapters 7-11

somewhat foolish in telling them such apparently egocentric dreams. They could have resented his arrogance, if that was what they thought it was. They could have written it all off as just an expression of their brother's wishful thinking. But they knew there was more to it than that. Something in the repetition of the dreams made them sit up and take notice. They reckoned it might be a divine message, and they were determined that it should not be fulfilled. Perhaps, knowing their family history, they recognised and believed that God had chosen Joseph to rule over them, and they were resistant to God's purpose. It seemed so unfair – after all, they were all older than young Joseph!

Like many today, these brothers found the doctrine of God's election obnoxious. God's election is connected to God's grace, that is, His will to choose and rescue and help and use unworthy people for their good and His glory. This is precisely the significance of the dreams. God's choice of Joseph provoked a reaction in his brothers. They resented it; they loathed the very idea that God should make such a choice. This is still the natural reaction of people who have no relationship with God to the idea of God's grace being God's choice! People react against it; they question God's character, doubt His justice and reject His purpose. This becomes all the clearer when we contrast it with Jacob's reaction. Even though he rebuked his favourite son for his brashness, as he saw it, in recounting the dreams, he nonetheless 'kept the saying in mind.'[8] He pondered it and mulled it over, and he treasured it in his heart. Just as Mary, the mother of our Lord treasured up the things the angels and shepherds and wise men saw and said,[9] so

---

[8] Genesis 37:11
[9] Luke 2:19

Jacob recognised that these dreams had come from God and contained truth. He may have been confused as to their meaning, but Jacob took these dreams seriously. He knew enough of God to do that. As we have already seen, God was revealing this at this early stage in the story to make it clear that Joseph's life experiences were not going to be the product of chance or fate. Everything that was going to happen subsequently would happen in the purpose of God.

Joseph's brothers also saw the point of his dreams and quite deliberately refused to accept the implications. Later on, in chapter 37:20, when they discuss killing the boy, they say, 'we will see what will become of his dreams.' They took the dreams seriously. These brothers could have bowed before God's will, accepting the discipline God intended, but instead they rejected God by rejecting Joseph. They were saying in effect that God's Word is not true and will not be true, and that they will make sure it never will be true. They were doing what the apostle Paul says everyone does naturally; they were 'suppressing the truth in unrighteousness' (to be unrighteous is to hate what is right by God's standard).[10] They were rejecting divine revelation and were determined to frustrate the designs of the Lord of hosts. This is one of the first instances in the Bible of man's natural response to the doctrine of election. Is it not still the case today that there are some things we will not let God talk to us about, and that there are some people through whom we will not let God speak to us?

---

[10] Romans 1:18

The trouble with envy

In addition to this rejection of divine revelation, a major character flaw is evident in these men, and that is their envy. Their actions have something to teach us about the true nature of envy. They did not just want what Joseph had; they wanted to ruin him altogether. Alvin Plantinga writes:

> *What the envier wants is not, first of all, what another has; what an envier wants is for another not to have it … To covet is to want someone else's good so strongly that one is tempted to steal it. To envy is to resent someone else's good so much that one is tempted to destroy it. The coveter has empty hands and wants to fill them with someone else's goods. The envier has empty hands and therefore wants to empty the hands of the envied. Envy, moreover, carries overtones of personal resentment: an envier resents not only someone else's blessing but also the one who has been blessed.*[11]

Envy is when I go beyond simply wanting the promotion to wanting my colleague not just to miss the opportunity to advance but lose their job altogether. Envy is bitter and nasty and out not just to *get*, but to *hurt*. This kind of envy breeds bitterness and provokes revenge.

Follow my leader

It is at this point that we are introduced to an inept leader. It is one of the features of Scripture that it frequently points out failure in leadership, whether leadership in the church, the home or the nation. Reuben was the eldest brother, the natural one to take the lead. He was already in real trouble with his father for having slept with his father's concubine Bilhah, so perhaps he was afraid of getting into even more

---

[11] A. Plantinga, *Not the Way it's Supposed to Be*, p162

trouble. For whatever reason, he makes a brave but flawed attempt at being a true leader:

'Let us not take his life.'[12]

Suddenly there is a door of hope for Joseph, for Scripture tells us that Reuben intended to come back and rescue the boy.[13] Reuben was at best half-hearted in his attempt to save Joseph, and he failed to take appropriate measures to ensure Joseph's safety. Good leaders leave nothing to chance. Once committed to a course of action, believing it to be right they see it through to the end. Reuben, however, left Joseph in the hands of men who were determined to kill him. His nerve failed him and he lost the day. Perhaps he didn't want to appear weak or the odd man out among his brothers. Reuben's failure of leadership here cost him the right of inheritance later.

This episode is a salutary warning to all leaders in church, state and commercial life. To be a leader involves making tough decisions; it means living with unpopularity; and it means (especially for a Christian) a fundamental commitment to practising integrity. It also involves an ability to manage the situation. For example, too many Christian leaders let things slip spiritually and doctrinally because they want to be liked or to be considered nice. They are easily driven by statistics and are afraid to make tough decisions when it comes to standing for truth. I remember someone saying to me at one church that he was afraid we were haemorrhaging numbers because of changes we were making. He didn't stay with us long enough to see that it

---

[12] Genesis 37: 21
[13] Genesis 37: 22

was a temporary blip on an upward trajectory. There is no doubt that while we were going through that period it was hard to hold it together, but a sense of principle and purpose required us to hold the line.

The language of the Genesis story suggests that his brothers brutally assaulted Joseph. They 'stripped him of his robe' like a bunch of wild animals tearing at his flesh as they tore it off him, 'cast him into a pit,' then proceeded to sit down and have their lunch. It was a cynical and callous action, leaving him to starve to death, having decided not to shed his blood. We cannot read Joseph's story at this point without thinking of the words spoken of Jesus, 'he came to his own and his own people did not receive him'.[14] In our story, the tragedy of what is happening is highlighted by the repetition of the word 'brother', which occurs twenty-one times in this chapter. It is all the more ironic when we see them sitting down eating their food whilst within earshot of their brother's cries for help and mercy. They are completely indifferent to his pleas. We know this from the brothers' own confession later on:

'we saw his distress of soul, when he begged us and we did not listen.'[15]

Much later in the history of God's people, this story was still in the mind of the prophet Amos when he warned the people of his day:

Woe to you...who drink wine in bowls...but are not grieved over the ruin of Joseph![16]

---

[14] John 1:11
[15] Genesis 42:21
[16] Amos 6:6

31

This was a horrible wickedness, but it highlights the intensity of their hatred. As Calvin comments with tongue in cheek, 'You know, seeing this family one knows why God graciously is sending Joseph to Egypt!'[17] Indeed! He needs to be well away from them!

When wrong seems right

Now that he was in the pit, Joseph was to be abandoned and left to starve, at the mercy of the elements; but providence was at work once more. A 'caravan of Ishmaelites' en route to Egypt came by.[18]

To one brother at least, the arrival of the merchants must have seemed fortuitous, because it is at this point that another brother, who is going to have a significant part to play in the ongoing drama of redemption, steps in. It seems that Reuben isn't around, so Judah comes up with the idea of selling Joseph to the traders. It is this suggestion which, in the providence of God, gets God's appointed saviour down to Egypt so that he can be the right man in the right place at the right time.

To Judah, it seemed the perfect solution! Here was a God-given opportunity to get rid of Joseph without actually harming him. There are many times in life when the wrong decision seems right to us. It seems right because it suits our purposes. Couples meet, they are married to other people, but in their loneliness they are thrown together. It seems so right. It is possible to rationalize away all the arguments we know against our course of action. The brothers were able to overcome any sense of guilt they may have had at killing Joseph by selling him to the Ishmaelites. So Joseph

[17] John Calvin, *Genesis*, Grand Rapids: Baker Book House 1979, 269
[18] Genesis 37:25

was sold for just 20 pieces of silver, the asking price for a slave in that region. Hardly a fortune, so it certainly wasn't done for financial gain. With hindsight, even the price was no coincidence. Jesus Himself would be betrayed for just 30 pieces of silver.

In the end it will be this same brother, eventually converted and transformed, who will be the ancestor of the Messiah. Jesus was to be born of Judah's line. There are parallels with the New Testament here. Matthew's Gospel tells us of another Joseph who goes down to Egypt to preserve the life of the chosen one, descended from Judah, who will be the saviour of Israel and the world.[19] This Genesis story shows us that the choice of Judah had nothing at all to do with any worthiness on his part, but was dependent purely on the grace of God. God's grace is always shown not to worthy achievers but to unworthy sinners. Judah most certainly isn't a worthy man at this point. He is definitely a sinner and yet God is going to use him for His glory. This is always the way of grace with us.

No doubt Judah would have defended his decision as being the 'right' thing to do in the circumstances. Perhaps he would have argued that it was the lesser of two evils, 'and the timing was perfect'! Later in the Old Testament Jonah the prophet is found running away from that one spot on the map where God said he should be.[20] One of the surprising things is that when he ran away he found a ship waiting to take him in the opposite direction! That must have seemed a case of circumstances confirming his course of action! He might even have convinced himself that God must be in the coincidence. Sometimes we too defend our compromises in

---

[19] Matthew 2:13-15
[20] Jonah 1:3

similar terms. When we have a heart to disobey God there is often the opportunity presented to do just that.

Where on earth is your God?
This chapter of Genesis raises questions about how much God is involved in these matters. His name is not mentioned, yet He is clearly 'unseen yet forever at hand.'[21] The father showed favouritism and the brothers' resentment grew into murderous hatred, and they bore complete responsibility for these attitudes. Yet it is still true that God was using the situation for His own purposes.

In the Westminster Confession of Faith we have a pretty comprehensive statement about God's providence:

> *God, the great Creator of all things, does uphold, direct, dispose, and govern all creatures, actions, and things, from the greatest even to the least, by his most wise and holy providence.*[22]

This passage talks about a number of factors: God's free will (He does what He chooses); the will of His creatures (they do what they choose within their power); and the effects of second causes (wars, storms, disease, famine etc). It expresses what is demonstrably shown in Joseph's story; that God ordains everything that comes to pass. The dreams right at the beginning of the story show that God is working to a script, His own script, written from eternity. By recounting these dreams, Joseph is announcing to his family what history will prove to be true, that God is in what happens next, overruling it to His own glory.

---

[21] A. Toplady, 'A sovereign protector I have'
[22] Westminster Confession of Faith V:I (Edinburgh: Free Church of Scotland, 1955), p10

No one can read the story of Joseph and seriously expect us to buy into the popular new theory known as 'Open Theism'. This talks about 'the openness of God,'[23] which says that God doesn't know the future but reacts to history as it happens. God acts without a script and He is as surprised by events as we are. This, they argue is necessary if God is to have integrity in His dealings with us. That is not the case here and it is not the uniform teaching of Scripture; rather God is guiding history according to His own plans. Yet, at the same time, people make their own free choices. God did not manipulate the brothers into hating Joseph. They did so freely, yet they served God's purposes of salvation. No-one made the Jews of Jesus' day hate the Messiah, but they did and they rejected Him and did away with Him, or so they thought. When Judas betrayed Jesus, it did not thwart God's purpose but served it. Though wicked men killed Him, it was what His counsel and will determined beforehand should happen. In other words, God really is God. His sovereignty and even His blessing can be found in the midst of the most heinous crimes and the most disastrous circumstances. This is not to say that He approves of the crimes or enjoys watching disaster, it is simply a testimony to the fact that God brings good out of evil while still holding us accountable for our decisions and actions.

When Joseph trudged off down the road to Egypt, his brothers probably thought they were at last done with him. When Reuben came back and found Joseph was no longer in the pit,[24] he must have felt totally helpless, which

---

[23] Richard Rice, John Sanders, Clark Pinnock and William Hasker, *The Openness of God: A Biblical Challenge to the Traditional Understanding of God*, Downers Grove IL, Inter Varsity Press

[24] Genesis 37:29

of course he was. When his father was told the concocted story about wild animals and saw the blood on the famous coat, he was inconsolable, but the brothers chose to perpetuate the lie and pretended to console their father.[25] What could have been more heartless and cynical? Yet sin is like this. Once we let it take a grip on our hearts it wants more and more control. It asserts itself until we are being driven further and further away from a place where we are able to respond to God. James writes:

> *Each person is tempted when he is lured and enticed by his own desire, then desire when it has conceived gives birth to sin, and sin when it is fully grown brings forth death.*[26]

Sin, unchallenged and unconfessed, makes us harder and less responsive until we can play any game, even a game of grief where there is none felt. It hardens our hearts till they are like granite.

And what of Joseph? We simply cannot imagine what he must have been going through. To be thrown in the pit and listen to his brothers' conversation about killing him; to be pulled up out of the pit 'expecting death' and then to be carted off in chains behind a group of foreign travellers to who knows where and to what uncertain fate – what a traumatic and terrifying experience! Yet Scripture insists that:

> *we know that for those who love God all things work together for good, for those who are called according to his purpose.*[27]

---

[25] Genesis 37:31-5
[26] James 1:15
[27] Romans 8:28

Joseph was assuredly 'called according to God's purpose.' He wasn't aware of it at that moment and there would be many more such moments, as we shall learn. But we know the end of the story. It is put in the Bible as a testimony to us. And it is an encouragement to those of us who are still somewhere on the road to Egypt, with hearts broken by the rejection of loved ones, feet blistered by the sharp rocks of affliction, and with a thousand questions racing through our heads and no answers in sight. The answer may not come on command any more than it came to Joseph on that hot and dusty road to Egypt. It may not come till we get home to heaven. But one day we will see the purpose of it all and rejoice in the wisdom of God, understanding at last that when we most thought He was absent, He was most near.

> *He hides himself so wondrously,*
> *As though there were no God;*
> *He is least seen when all the powers*
> *Of ill are most abroad.*

> *Thrice blest are they to whom is given*
> *The instinct that can tell*
> *That God is on the field when he*
> *Is most invisible.*

Frederick William Faber (1814-63)

3

An Indecent Proposal

The last we hear of Joseph in Genesis chapter 37 is that on arriving in Egypt he is sold as a slave to Potiphar, one of Pharaoh's officials and captain of the guard.[1] He must have felt heartbroken and terrified as he arrived in Egypt. The loss of home and family was enough to bear, without the additional trauma and pain of being rejected and ill-treated by his own brothers, but on top of that Joseph also has to deal with the humiliation of being put on public view and sold to the highest bidder. What will happen next? What will become of him? Will he ever see his family again? Would he want to? As with all good storytellers, the author leaves his readers on tenterhooks, anxious to hear what happens next.

A revealing interlude
The next scene in this drama (Genesis 38) answers none of

---

[1] Genesis 37:36

these questions. This unedifying episode concerning Judah is all about sex and violence and at first sight appears to be a random interruption to the story. Instead of following Joseph down the road to Egypt, Moses (the author) moves the scene moves back to Canaan, Joseph's homeland, and to what remains of his shabby family. If this were a movie, the caravan of camels would wind their way down towards Egypt, perhaps with some pyramids in the heat-shimmering distance, the scene would fade out; the cameras would cut back to a village in Canaan, and the title would appear at the bottom of the screen with that one word, 'Canaan'. So what is the author doing here? Why doesn't he get on with the story, and should we just skip Genesis 38?

The answer is that there is a *literary* reason for putting this story at this position in the narrative. Moses is not only writing history, he is also writing a literary narrative. Leland Ryken tells us that whereas a historian tells us what *happened,* a writer of literary narrative tells us *what* happened.[2] Moses is cranking up the tension. As we read the story of Judah and Tamar, the chief characters of this next scene, we keep thinking, 'I don't want to know about you, I want to know what is going on with Joseph.' At another level the writer is contrasting the behaviour of the two sons. Joseph has already appeared as a fine upstanding boy. His character is here being contrasted with this up-close-and-personal look at the character of his brother Judah. In this chapter Judah will succumb to sexual temptation, whilst in the next Joseph will resist this very same temptation.

There is also a *theological* reason for including this story. Early in the book of Genesis, as Adam and Eve face

---

[2] Leland Ryken, *How to Read the Bible as Literature*, p76

eviction from the Garden of Eden for disobeying God's command, they are given a promise that the woman's seed will one day destroy their deceiver, Satan. God then sets in motion a series of events that culminates in the coming of the Messiah. In particular, God initiates the covenant with Abraham, promising that he will become a great nation. It was in Egypt that this promise would come true as Jacob's sons and their families multiplied until there were so many of them that they became a threat to the stability of Egypt.[3] God also promises that through Abraham's seed all nations of the earth will be blessed. Joseph's story so far prompts the question, 'Can God really use *this* family to bring blessing to the world?'

In many ways this unedifying story of Judah and Tamar is one of the last things we might expect the Bible to record. Yet by including this story of God's dealings with Judah, Moses is giving us a further insight into the family from which first King David and then ultimately the Messiah would be descended. What a wonder that Jesus comes to be known by Judah's name, the Lion of the tribe of Judah![4] This story also shows us something about the mystery of God's providence. It is remarkable that God should work through such inauspicious events as these. The sad tale of Tamar and Judah confirms the fact that God often uses the most unlikely people, who come from less than perfect backgrounds, to accomplish His purposes for His glory. It may be that you feel your past is too messy, your family too dysfunctional, your record too unsatisfactory for God to be able to use you. But read this and be encouraged that nothing and no-one is impossible as far as God is concerned.

---

[3] Exodus 1:6-10

The slippery slope

Having seen the way these brothers treated Joseph, it might be thought that this family couldn't sink any lower, but it can and it will. Let no-one ever say that the Bible is unrealistic, or that it offers us a sanitised view of human life and behaviour. When we read it today, we find a world very different from ours in terms of technology and sociology, but it is no different in terms of morality and relationships.

This interlude in chapter 38, in which Joseph himself is never mentioned, allows the spotlight to fall on Judah, which is surprising since he was only son number-four in the family, one of Leah's children. Yet it is this man whom God, in His mysterious providence, is preparing to use. Up to now all we know of him is that when the caravan of Midianite traders appeared on the horizon in chapter 37, it was Joseph's half-brother Judah who came up with the idea of selling Joseph off to them rather than have his blood on their hands. What his motivation was in this we can only guess. Perhaps he had twinges of conscience about what they were doing and thought up a way to feel less guilty. They weren't actually going to kill Joseph and could make some money at the same time, although as has already been observed, 20 shekels wasn't exactly mega-bucks! Whatever Judah's motives, this next episode in the story finds him sinking even lower both morally and spiritually.

> *It happened at that time that Judah went down from his brothers and turned aside to a certain Adullamite whose name was Hirah.*[5]

---

[4] Revelation 5:5
[5] Genesis 38:1

Taken together, the two highlighted phrases tell us a lot about what was going on in Judah's life. He 'went down' geographically, but Moses is also stressing that he 'went down' spiritually. The expression to 'turn aside' is rarely used in Scripture of visiting a person or a place. It is usually used of someone who deviates from the path of loyalty and righteousness. It seems that Judah chose to leave home and stay with a Canaanite friend, Hirah. Does this indicate that he had already chosen to spend more time with Canaanites than with his brothers? Moses does not comment, but it is certainly true for us as Christians that we need to take heed if we prefer the company of unbelievers to that of our Christian brothers and sisters. Scripture does not tell us why Judah left home, but it may be that he could not cope with watching Jacob mourn for his beloved son, whom he believed to be dead. Perhaps Judah's conscience was troubling him again!

How far down was Judah going to go?

> *There Judah saw the daughter of a certain Canaanite whose name was Shua. He took her and went in to her.*[6]

This is exactly what the Hebrew says, he 'saw' and he 'took'. It has all the finesse of pure lust! Put those phrases together and we have the picture of a man who is in serious spiritual decline. He lives in the Promised Land, but instead of being a blessing in it, he just tries to fit in, to be like everyone else, and he conforms to the world and life-view of everyone around him. Judah's life was no different from that of the people of the nations around who did not follow the God of Abraham.

---

[6] Genesis 38:2

So we find a weakening of faith in God's chosen family. Once so strong in Abraham, faith seems to have declined steadily in just two generations. This is the way it goes in families today unless it is rekindled by a personal experience of God. We may have had committed Christian parents, but we can be cold and indifferent ourselves to the things of God. If that is the case, we need to have a fresh and personal encounter with the living God. Like many children of believers who leave the church and settle in the world, Judah leaves the Promised Land and settles among the Canaanites. He deliberately turns his back on the promises of God by turning away from the chosen family. Abraham had been called to be a blessing to the whole world, but Judah turns away from the one family on earth that God has chosen to bless. He copies his uncle Esau and marries an unbelieving or pagan wife, and he lives like a Canaanite. So will the covenant promise be thwarted? Will true faith die out?

Family matters
As the years go by, it must have seemed that God was blessing Judah. His marriage lasted, and three sons were born. However, it seems that not only did Judah fail as a believer, but he also failed as a father:

> *Er, Judah's firstborn, was wicked in the* LORD's *sight; so the* LORD *put him to death.*[7]

There may be some parents, whose children no longer walk with God, who have sensitive consciences and wonder if their children's rebellion is their fault. In the case of adult children, the children are accountable for their own choices

---

[7] Genesis 38:7

and actions. While they are in our care as youngsters, our responsibility is to bring them up in the care, knowledge and nurture of the Lord. The text tells us that Judah got a Canaanite wife for Er,[8] in other words he was a hands-on dad whose values were not at this stage godly values. When that is the case, it is quite possible to lead our children astray. I think of one person I knew whose supposedly Christian parents were pressing him to marry a suitable young lady who was not a Christian, indeed she was anti-Christian. Their Christian principles went out the window in favour of their ambition to have grandchildren!

The fate of Er is one of those rare places in the Bible when we are told straight out that the Lord put someone to death.[9] It reflects the steep moral decline that had taken place in Jacob's family. It also highlights God's judicial dealings with people. Sin brings a penalty, either now or later, for 'the wages of sin is death.'[10] It still is! What our race needs is a remedy for the penalty for sin. This theme of the penal consequences of sin runs right through the Bible. This always means that either we pay the penalty ourselves or someone else pays for us. This is precisely what the Bible picks up on in the prophets and New Testament when it talks about Christ taking on Himself the penalty he didn't deserve on behalf of His people.[11] Without this there would be no gospel, because this is humanity's greatest need.

When Er died, his brother Onan was told to go in, and 'do the duty of a brother-in-law to her, and raise up offspring' for his brother.[12] This seems like a strange arrangement to us,

---

[8] Genesis 38:5,6 Kesib is a Canaanite town and Tamar a Canaanite name
[9] eg. Acts 5:1-11
[10] Romans 3:23
[11] Isaiah 52-53; Romans 3:21ff
[12] Genesis 38:8

though it was both familiar and quite legal in the society of those times. It fell in line with the Leverite laws which were universal in the Middle East at that period. The word *leverite* comes from *levir*, a Latin word meaning 'husband's brother'. It was all about succession and inheritance. If a man died before he and his wife had been able to have a son, then his brother had the responsibility to have a son with her who would become heir to the late husband's name and estate, ensuring that his line would continue. Onan understood this; he 'knew that the offspring would not be his'.[13] For Onan it was a birthright issue. Er was the firstborn son and therefore was entitled to the birthright. If he had no male heir, that right would pass to Onan, but if Tamar were to have a son, the boy would inherit his father's estate. This is why Onan does what he can to avoid getting Tamar, his sister-in-law, pregnant. He sleeps with her but uses his own 'natural' form of birth control to avoid getting her pregnant. He disobeys in secret, thinking that no-one will find out, since Tamar was unlikely to talk about such an embarrassing subject. But his selfish action denies his deceased brother the opportunity of a name and an inheritance. God knows even the deepest secrets, however, for nothing is hidden from His sight. Inevitably, there are consequences for Onan's actions, and Onan too dies.

It is probably worth saying at this point that this incident tells us nothing about whether it is right or not for Christian couples to use contraception. The issue here is quite specific and cultural, it is not commented on in Scripture nor made into a rule. Couples have to use their own prayerful judgment in this area and it would be foolish and quite wrong to legislate on this matter.

---

[13] Genesis 38:9

Poor Tamar! She had now lost two husbands. Some might say she was careless! Others might suggest, more maliciously, that she was jinxed. It was common in those days for people to think, superstitiously, that women who were prone to be widows were witches. To her father-in-law, Judah, she was an embarrassing problem. Perhaps he thought that he might be next to die. He urges her to go home to her father's house and live there, as far away as possible from him and his family; after all he'd already lost two boys over this woman! He sends her off with the promise that when his next son, Shelah, comes of age; he will do the necessary and have children with her on behalf of her dead husbands.

In fact, in sending Tamar back to her family to live in isolation and disgrace, Judah was simply airbrushing her out of the family picture, sending her away in the hope that she would disappear quietly – out of sight, out of mind! This was a wicked thing for Judah to do, since it was his responsibility as head of the clan to care for the defenceless widow. He was violating his daughter-in-law by denying her rights, by not looking after her well-being, and by shunting her off to be looked after by others. The whole situation was a mess! Yet Moses wants us to see that God is at work through it all, despite appearances. To anyone looking on, there was no visible sign of God's presence in the situation, and things were going to get worse.

Tamar's revenge
As the years passed and Shelah grew to manhood, Tamar knew that Judah had reneged on his promise:

> *She saw that Shelah was grown up, and she had not been given to him in marriage.*[14]

---

[14] Genesis 38:14

What was she to do? Now, there is one thing we must say about Tamar, which is that she had remained loyal to Judah and his family for many years by this stage. During those long years – probably around twenty – she could have married another Canaanite man or become a cult prostitute in a Canaanite temple. She stands out in the Bible because whereas Canaanite women normally absorbed Israelite men into their pagan culture (as appears to have been the case with Judah's wife), she did the reverse. She chose to stick by her rather flawed in-laws and remained loyal to the memory of her first husband. It was this loyalty which drove her to undertake her daring plan.

After a period of mourning following his wife's death, Judah went up 'to Timnah to shear the sheep' with his old friend Hirah.[15] The NIV says it was Judah's men who were doing the shearing. Clearly this was a major event, a perfect excuse for a party. When Tamar hears about this she determines to get her father-in-law to do the right thing by fair means or foul, so that Er's honour can be upheld. What a sad commentary on Judah's reputation that his daughter-in-law could be confident that she could get the better of him by posing as a prostitute, for that is precisely what she did!

She took off her widows garments and covered herself with a veil, wrapping herself up, and sat at the entrance to Enaim, which is on the road to Timnah.[16]

What was Tamar up to? Cult prostitution was an essential part of Canaanite religion. As part of the process

---

[15] Genesis 38:12
[16] Genesis 38:14

of invoking the gods to make their flocks, wives or lands productive and fruitful, people engaged in ritual sex with temple prostitutes. It would therefore have been no surprise to Judah to find a cult prostitute on the outskirts of the village of Enaim. Tamar knew her man well. This incident gives a glimpse into just how absorbed Judah had become into the culture into which he had married. He was to all intents and purposes a Canaanite. It is a warning to those of us who claim to be God's people. We should be careful whom we marry. Will our chosen spouse help or hinder our spiritual life and growth? It is also a warning that we should be careful how much we buy into the values of the world around us. That route can lead to spiritual disaster.

Judah can't pass up the opportunity of a fling, even though he doesn't have his equivalent of a credit card with him to pay for her services. Tamar has already thought through all of this very shrewdly, and insists that he leave her a guarantee of payment in the form of his signet, cord and staff.[17] Each of these items was of great significance. The signet was a stamp seal, with an engraved design on it identifying Judah. It was worn on a cord around the neck and would have been used for any major purchase, transaction or correspondence, much as we would use a signature today. The staff was his symbol of authority in the clan. This woman has stitched him up big time! Although the text stresses that Judah was not aware he was sleeping with his daughter-in-law, nonetheless he does, and Moses simply records the incident without moral comment. In the next chapter, by contrast, he will tell how Joseph behaves properly in sexual matters.

---

[17] Genesis 38:18

The road to repentance

Well, this risky strategy wins through, and Tamar 'conceived by him'.[18] Since the Bible teaches that it is the Lord who opens the womb, we see His hand using a bad set of circumstances to accomplish His will. People are responsible for their own actions, but God is well able to overrule and overturn human intentions to serve His will. Three months later, when Judah is told that his daughter-in-law is pregnant and that she must have engaged in prostitution, he is furious.

Judah said, 'Bring her out and have her burned to death.'[19]

It is galling to see the double standard at work here. There is one law for men and another for women! Here was a man who didn't hesitate to use a cult prostitute, yet who was prepared to burn this woman for supposedly acting in the same way he had. Here is one wicked fornicator who is quick to condemn another for the same crime. His language is brutal and decisive. There is no question of giving her a hearing; this is one way to get rid of the irritant once and for all! But Tamar has an ace up her sleeve:

> *'By the man who owns these I am pregnant,' she said. And she added, 'Please identify whose these are, the signet and the cord and the staff.'[20]*

Judah cannot deny that these items belong to him, and is publicly exposed for his folly.

The effect on Judah is immediate:

> *Then Judah identified them and said, 'She is more righteous than I, since I did not give to her my son Shelah.'*

---

[18] Genesis 38:18
[19] Genesis 38:24
[20] Genesis 38:25

And he showed he had learned a lesson, for he 'did not know her again.'[21] She is righteous! The term is a forensic one; it has nothing to do with her ethnic status (she was not an Israelite) but with her legal status. Tamar had done the right thing, but Judah was in the wrong. Tamar becomes a hero in Israel because she was prepared to take risks to perpetuate her husband's name and line.

For the first time in the narrative we find a chink in Judah's armour. This public exposure touches something deep within him. He is convicted of sin and he says so. His confession of sin is a sign that God is working within him. It is always this way. In the New Testament the apostle John says:

> *if we say we have no sin, we deceive ourselves, and the truth is not in us. If we confess our sins, he is faithful and just to forgive us our sins and to cleanse us from all unrighteousness.*[22]

Judah confesses his sin and the first step is taken towards a transformation in this man's life. His story, like that of his great descendant David, takes a turn for the better when he admits his sin.[23] And no doubt, like David, he is forgiven, for God forgives those who repent, and his repentance is real, for he 'did not know her again.'

Judah's destiny is wrapped up in his relationship to Tamar. As a result of this incestuous and lustful affair, Tamar bears twins. Astonishingly, this marks Judah out as the one who would succeed his father as the leading patriarch. And just as there was conflict in the womb between his father and uncle, Jacob and Esau, so there is conflict in Tamar's womb as the boys are born.

---

[21] Genesis 38:26
[22] 1 John 1:8-9
[23] 2 Samuel 12:13

When she was in labour, one put out a hand, and the midwife took and tied a scarlet thread on his hand, saying, 'This one came out first.' But as he drew back his hand, behold, his brother came out.[24]

The firstborn's name was Perez, founder of the line from which David the king and ultimately the Messiah was to be born.

In Matthew's genealogy of Christ, only five women are mentioned.[25] They are Tamar, Rahab, Ruth, Bathsheba, and Mary. Tamar posed as a prostitute, Rahab was a prostitute, Ruth was a pagan Moabitess, Bathsheba was an adulteress, and Mary was wrongly regarded as immoral because no-one would believe her story. It is a pointer to the humility and grace of the Messiah that He should choose to be identified with such as these. Tamar's persistence in fulfilling this cultural demand that her first husband have an heir ensured that the one Person who could actually deal with human sin would come into the world.

In Revelation 5, when all heaven is gathered to hear who it is that is worthy to take the scroll, open the book and supervise the unfolding of human history, John weeps because no-one is found. Then one of the heavenly elders says to him:

Weep no more; behold, the Lion of the tribe of Judah, the Root of David, has conquered, so that he can open the scrolls and its seven seals.[26]

John turns to look for this kingly conqueror and sees the Lord Jesus, exalted and seated on the throne of the universe.

---

[24] Genesis 38:28-30
[25] Matthew 1:3, 5, 6, 16
[26] Revelation 5:5

On a human level, it all goes back to this scandalous one-night stand with a prostitute!

The next time we see Judah in this story he will be a prince among his brothers, willing to sacrifice himself rather than his youngest step-brother, the chief carer for his father and willing to die so that his family may be spared. As such, he becomes a type of Christ, his greatest descendant, who would give His life as a ransom for many. At the end of the story, Judah is a saint, and he becomes the founder of the royal line. It is a signal of the change which will occur in this man that in Revelation his name is written 'on the gates of the heavenly Jerusalem.'[27] You see, even the worst of sinners can enter heaven by God's redeeming grace. He saves by grace and not by merit. This truth teaches us to delight in the gracious love of God that chooses and saves unworthy sinners, and it teaches us to thank God for these biblical examples of fallen saints, whose stories invite us back to God from our wanderings.

It may well be that there are skeletons in your cupboard and scandals you are running from. Yet do not doubt that God can both save you and use you, whether you are an incest survivor like Tamar, or an immoral failure like Judah. People can change, and God is in the business of making all things new.

---

[27] Revelation 21:12

4

Fatal Attraction

As we come to this new scene in the drama of Joseph's life, it is important to remind ourselves of its place in the overall story. Having learned about the betrayal and sale of Joseph, we had expected to immediately find out his fate. Instead Moses took us back to Canaan and introduced us more fully to the character of Judah, whose story plays a vital part in the outworking of God's covenant with Abraham. As anyone who reads the end of the story will see, it is through Judah that the promise of the coming Messiah is to be carried on. At this stage, however, Judah seems completely unworthy and unreliable. He has been responsible for his brother's disappearance. One sin has led to another, there has been a steady moral as well as spiritual decline, and now he is involved in a case of incest. The key to the significance of that story in Judah's life lies in his confession when confronted with Tamar's real identity and story: 'She is more righteous than I.'[1] That

---

[1] Genesis 38:26

is a very important admission. It points us to the beginning of a fundamental change in this man, a transformation which will become complete through his contact with the hero of our story.

But what has happened to Joseph? The opening of chapter 39, 'Now Joseph had been brought down to Egypt,' resumes the account of Joseph, someone who acts righteously in the very area of life in which Judah had sinned and who, 'in accordance with God's plan,'[2] is to become the saviour of Judah, and indeed of all his family. Judah had gone down to the Canaanites and become like them in their immorality, whilst Joseph is brought down to Egypt against his will but does not adopt the lifestyle and moral attitudes of the Egyptians. He doesn't lose his identity as one of God's people. His very integrity opens doors that will eventually lead to the highest position in the land, putting him in the very place where God can make a difference and be the one to rescue and provide for his people.

God at work

In this chapter we shall see something of the godliness of Joseph, although that is not a theme which is found in relation to him in Scripture. Nowhere is he held up as a moral example. No exhortations are based on his life in Scripture. Moses does not urge us to go and live a life like Joseph's. His life's true significance rests in the larger purposes of God.

Chapter 39 opens with the news that Joseph survives the arduous journey to Egypt and is sold into slavery, for

---

[2] Genesis 45:5

'Potiphar, an officer of Pharaoh, the captain of the guard, an Egyptian, had bought him from the Ishmaelites'.[3] We can only imagine the absolute humiliation of being put up for auction in the public square. Here is this young man who had been given a privileged status by his folks at home now being treated as a non-person. As he stood on the dais being inspected for fleas or lice, being prodded and pushed around, he must have feared what kind of master he would end up with, and felt anxious about the future. Is this further bad news for Joseph? No, for there is a clear signal in the text that this is a good outcome and that God is in it, for 'the LORD was with Joseph.'.[4] Things are about to take a positive turn. It is good to be told this, because that's not the way his circumstances appear as the next part of the story unfolds!

It would be easy to glide over the information that God was with Joseph as if it were a kind of spiritual gloss on the story, just a pious nicety. But there is more to it than that. In Psalm 105 we are called to remember 'the wondrous works that [the LORD] has done.' The Psalmist immediately goes on to talk about the 'covenant', that special and binding arrangement which God had made with Abraham, promising him a family ('seed') and a land as his inheritance. Ultimately this promise was to be fulfilled in the Messiah, Jesus, but there was a tortuous journey to be taken until it could be worked out in history. As the Psalmist recalls the flow of history in the working out of this promise, he says that the Lord 'sent a man ahead of them [that is, Israel, the bearer of the promise], Joseph who was sold as a slave.'[5] The main actor in the drama

---

[3] Genesis 39:1
[4] Genesis 39:2
[5] Psalm 105:5, 8-9, 17

is therefore God, and the underlying theme is the unfolding purposes of God, especially His keeping of His covenant promise to Abraham. Joseph's role is to be God's man in the right place at the right time. God had sent a man 'ahead of them'. The God of the Bible not only knows the future, He plans and shapes the future for His own glory.

A profitable servant

The journey down to Egypt would have been fascinating. Joseph had come a long way from the rural farmlands of home to the rich and sophisticated urban heartland of the world's superpower of the day. As he was led along the Nile valley, he would have seen the Pyramids in their heyday; they were newly built in that period. All around he would have seen and heard evidence of Egypt's multiple gods. As well as local deities, he would have heard of the cosmic gods, like Ra, the sun god, and Nut the sky goddess. He would have heard of the cult of Osiris and of the divine Pharaoh himself. The name of his new master, Potiphar, meant *'he whom Ra (the sun god) has given'*. He had come to a strangely cosmopolitan and pluralist society, where there were so many gods but no knowledge of his God. Yet it was not Ra who was in charge of Egypt and Joseph's destiny, it was Yahweh, the God of Israel who is the Lord of the whole earth.

The story begins unexpectedly with Joseph making an immediate impression on his new boss. It isn't long before he is making strides along his career path. He is being given more and more responsibility:

> *he became a successful man, and he was in the house of his Egyptian master.*[6]

[6] Genesis 39:2

This means that he quickly rose out of the ranks of general slave to that of a household slave.[7] This was far better than working outdoors under the searing Egyptian sun.

Why was he so successful? Joseph was a faithful witness to his Lord while he lived with Potiphar.

His master saw that the LORD was with him and that the LORD caused all that he did to succeed in his hands.[8]

This implies that his master knew of his religious convictions. He had not been totally quiet about where he had come from or about whose authority he recognised in his life. This raises a question for those of us who are Christians. Are we clear in our profession of Christ? Apparently Joseph was able to bear witness clearly without alienating his employer because of the transparent integrity of his life. Alexander MacLaren once said:

> *The best advertisement of Christianity is a good life. People read us a great deal more than they read the Bible.*[9]

The key word in this story is the word LORD; it is used eight times in chapter 39.[10] When it is printed in upper case letters in our Bible, it translates God's personal name, his covenant name, Yahweh. It intentionally calls to mind the promises made to Joseph's great-grandfather Abraham. What are we told about the LORD? Four times we are told that 'the LORD was with Joseph'.[11] In all his troubles, in spite of rejection and his being sold into slavery and carted off into a foreign land, God's relationship and faithfulness to

---

[7] The word for house is repeated five times to emphasise this
[8] Genesis 39:3
[9] Cited in John D. Currid, *Genesis*, (Evangelical Press) p225
[10] Genesis 39:2 (twice); 3 (twice); 21 (once); 23 (twice).
[11] Genesis 39:2; 3; 21; 23

him never changed. This should be no surprise to anyone who reads Genesis, for one of the themes of the book is the pledge of God, 'I will be with you.' God had appeared to Isaac and said, 'Fear not, for I am with you.'[12] And when Joseph's father Jacob was far from home and had a dream of a ladder stretching down to him from heaven, God had given him the reassurance, 'Behold, I am with you.'[13] The presence of God suggests primarily a personal relationship. God was with Joseph in Egypt.

God of surprises

This would have had an impact on those who first read this book. Moses would have written this account in the wilderness as he led the people to the Promised Land. Memories of their 400-plus years in Egypt were raw. The Israelites still could remember the lashes and the hard labour and the oppression of living there. The very name was burned into their minds as a symbol of the world which is opposed to God's people. Surely there was nothing good or positive you could say about Egypt? Yet they couldn't have ignored the fact that in Moses' narrative God's name is not mentioned at all in the record of Joseph in Canaan. He doesn't make an entrance until Moses is talking about Joseph in Egypt; after that he is mentioned over and over! This teaches us that God will be with his people even in the most difficult and ungodly of circumstances. In the New Testament, Stephen, the first Christian martyr, reminds us of this very point:

---

[12] Genesis 26:24
[13] Genesis 28:15

And the Patriarchs, jealous of Joseph, sold him into Egypt, but God was with him.[14]

The conclusion Stephen draws from this is that their God is no tribal deity. He is not tied to any piece of real estate anywhere. He is not tied to the Promised Land or to the temple, indeed, "the Most High does not dwell in houses made by human hands." [15]

Jesus where'er your people meet
There they behold your mercy seat
Where'er they seek you, you are found
And every spot is hallowed ground.[16]

Since the earth is the Lord's, we can go out to win it for Him.

Although all that Joseph could see in Egypt were the altars, shrines, statues, graffiti, murals, stonework, monuments, wristbands and jewellery, all dedicated to a multiplicity of false gods, yet even there the living God was with him. Although he could see precious little evidence of God in his own life so far, in his own family or in his present circumstances, nonetheless God was going to use him to fulfil his promise to Abraham. Joseph was to be a blessing to this pagan nation, Egypt, and to his own family, but first God was going to bless Potiphar through Joseph.

First 'Joseph found favour' in his master's sight, then he was appointed Potiphar's personal assistant and eventually put in charge of his entire household.

---

[14] Acts 7:9
[15] Acts 7:48
[16] William Cowper

The blessing of the LORD was on all that he had, in house and field. So he left all that he had in Joseph's charge.[17]

This blessing of Potiphar is a foretaste of the blessing that eventually was to come to the whole world through the ultimate covenant man, the Lord Jesus, Abraham's seed according to promise. Our Lord Jesus not only had God with him as Joseph did, but God was in Christ, and His coming meant blessing for the whole world. He is present today with His people, and wherever they are different from the world, they bless the world.

When evangelical revival broke out in eighteenth-century England, society was degenerate and inexorably moving towards a bloody revolution. The revival produced tens of thousands of Christian people and things began to change in society at large. Civility was introduced into society; slavery was abolished; child labour ended; respect for the property of others became important; and the foundations of modern democracy were laid. It is yet to be seen whether democracy or decency survive the current decline of Christian influence in the West!

The power of lust

For a while, it seems, all was going well in Joseph's new life in Egypt, but Joseph was about to discover that he was unwittingly becoming the cause of his own downfall. Scripture tells us that 'Joseph was handsome in form and appearance'.[18] Apparently it was in the genes, for this phrase is used only in one other place in the Bible, and that is of his mother, Rachel![19] He must have been a magnificent

---

[17] Genesis 39:5-6
[18] Genesis 39:6
[19] Genesis 29:17

specimen of manhood, but being good-looking makes someone both visible and vulnerable.

As the story is told in Genesis, Joseph apparently had no warning of trouble ahead. There was no build up, it was a straight demand:

> *after a time his master's wife cast her eye on Joseph and said, "Lie with me."*[20]

Her motivation is undisguised lust, her language is coarse and brazen, and her attentions are persistent 'day after day'.[21] She is besieging the man with her overtures, she will not take 'no' for an answer. She tries coming on strong, then, when that doesn't work, she tries coaxing him tenderly. She uses every weapon in her armoury; she is caught up in a vortex of lust. Yet every day he turns her down:

> *he would not listen to her, to lie beside her or to be with her.*[22]

It is only those who have resisted temptation who know its true power. Too many of us fall before we feel its full impact. In this Joseph points to Jesus. Our Lord was 'tempted in all points just as we are, yet without sin'.[23] It is no excuse for us to say, 'Well, he was perfect and could not sin.' The sheer intensity of the assault; the pressure to give way, the inducements to succumb to the devil's tests were far greater in Christ's case than anything we will ever experience simply because he resisted them.

---

[20] Genesis 39:7
[21] Genesis 39:10
[22] Genesis 39:10
[23] Hebrews 4:15

Far from meaning a shorter, painless struggle with temptation it involved Him in protracted resistance. Precisely because He did not yield too easily and was not like us, easy prey, the devil had to deploy all his wiles and use all his resources. The very fact that He was invincible meant that He endured the full force of temptation's ferocity, until hell slunk away, defeated and exhausted. Against us, a little temptation suffices. Against Him, Satan found himself forced to push himself to his limits.[24]

Joseph's example ought to cut us to the heart. It would have been neither easy for him as a man, nor safe for him as a slave to resist her. He could have reasoned that it was a small price to pay to keep his job; after all this was a powerful and influential woman. He could have argued with himself that in fact it might be to his advantage, it might get him even further up the vocational ladder. Or he might have given in to his raging hormones and thought, 'Well, why not, I can't help myself!' Such are our sinful human hearts that so often we can find good reasons for doing anything we really want to when the temptation is strong.

'But he refused'; and having refused he witnessed once more to the truth:

> *'Behold, because of me my master has no concern about anything in the house, and he has put everything that he has in my charge. He is not greater in his house than I am, nor has he kept back anything from me except yourself, because you are his wife. How then can I do this great wickedness and sin against God?'[25]*

Here is the Word of God at work in Egypt as Joseph speaks out against sin. When our Lord came as the Word

[24] Donald MacLeod, *The Person of Christ*, 227
[25] Genesis 39:8-9

made flesh, he came to bear witness to the law of God. He exposed the sinfulness of the human heart by showing us that sin has to do with lust as much as illicit sex; with coveting as much as stealing; and with hatred as much as murder.

What is significant for us is the way Joseph argues with Potiphar's wife. He refuses to sleep with her because of the trust placed in him – 'Behold, because of me my master has no concern about anything in the house, and he has put everything that he has in my charge.' Then he speaks to her about her husband – 'He is not greater in his house than I am, nor has he kept back anything from me except yourself, because you are his wife.' Then he talks about his loyalty to God – 'How then can I do this great wickedness and sin against God?' You can see that he took this issue seriously. It was a big deal to him. He calls the action evil; it would have been a 'great wickedness'.

James Boice says that 'one of the devil's tricks in his campaign to promote sin and limit godliness is to call sin something other than what it is and thus make it sound less objectionable and perhaps even desirable'.[26] So people talk about 'finding themselves'. or having a 'mid-life crisis', or they use euphemisms like 'having a bit on the side'. I remember one lady telling me that she was leaving her family because for years she had cleaned and cooked for them and now it was her time to 'get a life', to have some 'me time'! She even said she had prayed about it and 'had peace'. What would Joseph have told her? That it was a great wickedness, and all my excuses and yours fall down before the sinfulness of sin.

---

[26] James Montgomery Boice, *Genesis* Volume 3, 63

Joseph also calls it a breach of trust, for sin always affects other people. He says that his master had given him everything but one thing. There is an echo here of Adam and Eve in Eden, where our first parents were literally given everything but one thing. They were in a covenant relationship with God. A covenant has both a legal and a relational aspect to it, promises are made and trust is called for. When the devil emphasised that one thing and suggested God was being unfair, first Eve then Adam reached out for that 'one thing'.[27] Here Joseph uses the concept of trust and keeping promises as an argument against taking the one thing his master had withheld from him. Joseph saw that ultimately sin is an offence against God. To commit adultery would be to 'sin against God'. Many years later, King David understood this when he finally faced up to all the sin which resulted from his adultery with Bathsheba:

"Against you, you only, have I sinned and done what is evil in your sight."[28]

When we sin, we not only offend God but we also break his heart. C. H. Spurgeon commented on this:

While I regarded God as a tyrant, I thought sin a trifle; but when I knew him to be my Father, then I mourned that I had ever kicked against him. When I thought that God was hard, I found it easy to sin; but when I found God so kind, so good, so overflowing with compassion, I smote my breast to think that I could ever have rebelled against the one who loved me so, and sought my good.[29]

---

[27] Genesis 3:1-7

[28] Psalm 51:4. The story is recorded in 2 Samuel chapters 11 and 12

[29] Spurgeon, *Metropolitan Tabernacle Pulpit*, Volume 41, 304

What can we learn from the way Joseph resists sin? He sees himself as caught up in a series of interlocking levels of accountability. He owes it to his boss, to his God and to himself not to do this wicked thing. There is nobility in this man, both in his heart for God and in his loyalty towards those who trust in him. You can see that right here there is a world of difference to the 'me-centred' lives we live today. When making our moral or ethical decisions, we usually don't move much beyond our passions or our cravings. We make ourselves the centre of our world and decide accordingly. Martin Luther once defined sin as '*homo incurvatus in se*,' 'man curved in on himself'.[30] Perhaps we need to ask what mental games we are playing with ourselves to excuse or defend our behaviour.

Fleeing temptation

Temptation cannot be avoided in this life, but it is possible to resist it. Resistance begins with the mind. Joseph gives a clue by the way he had thought about such things beforehand. That prepared him for the ultimate test. There came a day when he was cornered.

> But one day, when he went into the house to do his work and none of the men of the house was there in the house, she caught him by his garment, saying, 'Lie with me.'[31]

Doing the right thing doesn't always mean you avoid difficulties or unfair consequences, however. The apostle Paul said that 'all who desire to live a godly life in Christ Jesus will be persecuted.'[32] Even a life lived in the presence

---

[30] Matt Jenson, *The Gravity of Sin: Augustine, Luther and Barth on homo incurvatus in se* (London: T&T Clark, 2007), 202 pp.

[31] Genesis 39:11-12a

[32] 2 Timothy 3:12

of God, with the assurance of His care and guidance, is a life lived at great risk.

And Joseph's master took him and put him into the prison.[33]

There are two aspects to this persecution First, there are false accusations and then there is the imprisonment. I'm sure you know the old saying, 'hell hath no fury like a woman scorned, nor having a rage like love to hatred turned.'[34] So the one who wanted to sleep with him now becomes vindictive against him. The false accusations are repeated twice as the tension is heightened and the shameful charges are levelled against God's man, once to the other servants and then to her husband Potiphar.[35]

The repetition of the phrase 'he forced me to'[36] presses home the injustice of it all. She talks to the other slaves in order to get witnesses to support her claim. Her use of the term 'Hebrew' is probably intended to play on their resentment of a foreigner being given such power over them. There is a smell of sulphur in the room, for behind this woman we hear the voice of another who is called 'the accuser of the brothers,' our old 'adversary the devil.'[37]

Understandably, Potiphar is absolutely seething when he hears the news. He's angry about the circumstances, he's angry at Joseph, he's angry because he has lost a good and trustworthy worker. Unsurprisingly, Joseph had no opportunity to defend himself. But I wonder too, could

---

[33] Genesis 39:20

[34] William Congreve, *The Mourning Bride*, III viii

[35] Genesis 39:14 and 17

[36] Once by the narrator (39:10-12) twice to her servants (39:13-15) and then to his master (39:16-18)

[37] Revelation 12:10; 1 Peter 5:8

Potiphar perhaps be suspicious of his wife's motives in telling him? The fact that Joseph was imprisoned might suggest this interpretation, because in Egypt attempted rape was a capital offence, so Potiphar could have had him executed.

The king's prisoner

Joseph was put into the king's prison. It is interesting to note that in the ancient Near East it is only in Egypt that there are records of anyone being put in jail. This is an instance where it can be demonstrated that the Bible accurately reflects the culture of the period. Being in prison at that period was not likely to be pleasant. Psalm 105:18 captures the cruelty of Joseph's experience. He was held like a caged animal:

> His feet were hurt with fetters; his neck was put in a collar of iron.

There are times in life when we wonder whether it is worth the bother to be good. I have known men in business who have done the right thing, but they have not benefited from it. Others have lost promotion, or been made redundant, and in some cases people have lost their reputation because the dogs were unleashed against them. In the history of the church, not all who chose to do the right thing saw any visible fruit for their troubles. Some were put in prison and ended their lives there.

There is a pattern to Joseph's life that has a ring of destiny to it. It is always God's way to make His people like Jesus, and we see Jesus in Joseph's story. There is this pattern of exaltation – humiliation – exaltation. It is precisely the pattern we see in the life of our Lord Jesus – from the throne to the cross to the throne again. He leaves the glory

He shared with the Father and humbles Himself to take on our humanity and then our sin. We find Him being misrepresented and mistreated just as Joseph was. The Bible talks about all the unrighteous things that unrighteous people said about Him. Then after experiencing the curse of the cross and separation from His Father, He is placed in ignominy in a grave. To the world looking on it was the final indignity. Yet three days later He is raised from the dead and is now exalted to His Father's right hand of power, with all authority in heaven and earth belonging to Him.

We should not be surprised when we read of a godly man being persecuted. Jesus told His followers, 'If they persecuted me, they will persecute you,'[38] and He taught His followers to see in this the blessing and favour of God Himself:

> Blessed are you when others revile you and persecute you and utter all kinds of evil against you falsely on my account. Rejoice and be glad, for your reward is great in heaven, for so they persecuted the prophets who were before you.[39]

The New Testament encourages us to 'consider [Jesus] who endured from sinners such hostility against Himself, so that you may not grow weary or faint-hearted.'[40]

Looking ahead to the end of the chapter, it becomes very clear that 'the LORD was with Joseph and showed Him steadfast love and gave Him favour in the sight of the keeper of the prison.'[41] God does not helicopter Joseph out of

---

[38] John 15:20
[39] Matthew 5:11-12
[40] Hebrews 12:3
[41] Genesis 39:21

trouble, but He remains with him in it. Here the covenant word (*hesed*) is used; it means 'kindness,' or 'steadfast love'. It means to act with love and loyalty to help a covenant partner in need. Jesus' name means 'Yahweh saves'. He is the LORD. He is also called Immanuel, meaning 'God is with us', and He promised, 'I am with you always, to the end of the age.'[42]

It is as though Moses is providing a voice-over to the storyline when he emphasises that God was with Joseph. Young Joseph didn't actually hear those words ringing in his ears as he was led to the prison. Perhaps sometimes as a child you would imagine something happening, you would play a part with your friends, and as you did so you imagined the music playing in the background as it does in a Hollywood movie. Of course real life is not like that. But if, when we get to heaven, a movie of our life was to be played back to us, there might be all kinds of dramatic music to accompany the different scenes. In the course of the story there will be moments you will remember and realise that when you were going through it for real you felt alone or unloved, or perhaps it seemed that everything was out of control. Then the voice-over will remind you of something you had missed: 'that meeting was no mere chance,' or 'that accident was no mistake,' for the LORD was with you there, and there, and then, and He has never left you nor forsaken you.

---

[42] Matthew 28:20

5

When Life Closes In

Life doesn't always go in a straight line. If A is the starting point, we often don't seem to get to B in a straight line. This can be true of our career path; it can be true of some of life's ambitions; and it is certainly often true of love relationships. A story I read in the paper recently illustrates the old adage that 'the course of true love never did run smooth'![1] It told of one couple who had met and dated in their teens only to lose touch with each other until they were in their mid-thirties. They reconnected, fell in love and now are happily married with a brood of children.

On our honeymoon, my wife Christine and I spent a very hot summer afternoon in Kew Gardens in London. I had dragged her around some of the more famous ecclesiastical establishments in the city, and as we sat on the grass, I told her that I'd recently read the story of a famous church in

---

[1] Shakespeare, *A Midsummer Night's Dream*

the area, Duke Street in Richmond. When I suggested that it must be close at hand and we should go to take a look, the idea was quickly squashed, but looking back I have often wondered at how amazingly accommodating new brides can be! In fact, it would be 27 years before I ever visited Duke Street, only to be called to be its pastor. Life doesn't always go in a straight line.

Surviving by faith

Life certainly wasn't straightforward for Joseph either. There were twists and turns and ups and downs on the road to his destiny, and chapter 40 tells us of one of the low points. How low can things go? Apparently pretty low indeed! We sometimes talk about someone's life being 'the pits'. Joseph's life is in the pits literally. He has been attacked, bound and thrown into a pit by his brothers, sold into slavery for 20 pieces of silver and then sold on as a slave. Now he has been falsely accused of adultery and thrown into a prison, a prison no better than a pit – in fact the same word is used of both the literal pit and the prison where he now finds himself. You would have thought that taking a stand for righteousness and witnessing to the truth would bring him blessing, but instead it leads to his persecution and imprisonment.

We have a hint of what is going on from Psalm 105:

Until what he said came to pass the word of the Lord tested him.[2]

The word of the Lord had come through Joseph's early dreams. In those, God had held out to him His purpose, but the fulfilment hadn't come right away. His hope was

---

[2] Psalm 105:19

hope deferred. So we find him learning to wait on God, in order to prove Him 'faithful who had promised'.[3]

Of course we know why Joseph is in this situation. At least we do if we take a quick squint at the end of the story, although as Moses writes this, he is careful to maintain the tension right through. He means us to ask questions: 'What is going on in this man's life?' 'Is there any sense to it?' 'Will any good come out of it?' There are tantalising moments of hope in this story. Joseph finds himself sold to a very important and powerful man who, finding him to be a good and faithful servant, gives him increasing responsibilities. Life seems to be getting better. Then, all change, as Mrs P makes her play for his attentions but then goes out of her way to make sure he pays for it heavily when she is rebuffed. So, we find Joseph is thrown in prison. Psalm 105 says of his time in prison that he is shackled like the other criminals. Things were bad enough when he was sold as a slave, but now he is being treated as a criminal.

However, God doesn't desert Joseph. He is with him in prison. At the end of chapter 39 we read:

the LORD was with Joseph and showed him steadfast love.[4]

God doesn't remove His man from the suffering, in fact at one level things just got worse, but He remains with him in the midst of it. In that prison God is preparing him for his destiny. He even puts Joseph in prison with the right people. In every detail of our lives, including those which superficially at least seem most out of control, God is working out His purpose. Moses is giving us this

---

[3] Hebrews 11:11
[4] Genesis 39:21

theological key to the story, but Joseph didn't have those words of reassurance to go on. He had to go by faith, just as we do.

Genesis has been painting a portrait of God's character. He is the true hero of the story. Presented as the creator, preserver and saviour of His people, He is active in creation, providence and redemption. This whole section at the end of Genesis is teaching us that history is in His hands; both the large-scale histories of peoples and nations, and the small-scale histories of individuals. This God has a plan and He is working to a script. We need to keep this in mind as we continue through this drama. For, as I pointed out in an earlier chapter,[5] it is precisely in this area that the God of the Bible is being attacked by some from within the evangelical community today. Advocates of 'Open Theism' want to say that God doesn't know the future in any meaningful sense. Certainly they dislike the idea that He has planned it. They say He is in the process of discovery and 'becoming' just as we are. He certainly makes better guesses than we do, but He is 'reacting' to circumstances, not shaping them. Such ideas are clearly contradicted by the story of Joseph. In Joseph's own words to his brothers, which form Moses' own explanation of events, 'you meant it for evil, God meant it for good.'[6] 'Meant it,' notice; nothing took God by surprise. The free decisions of these men served His purposes after all. We need to keep this in mind as we move on to see this next episode in his life.

The butler, the baker, the destiny maker
Chapter 40 begins with a time reference, 'Some time

---

[5] See chapter 2, p. 35
[6] Genesis 50:20

later ....' It is now over ten years since Joseph was sold into slavery. The total period of his slavery and imprisonment will be thirteen years.[7] We are told that after he is put in prison two other prisoners join him, Pharaoh's chief cupbearer and chief baker. These men occupied important roles at court. Archaeology confirms that such individuals were often wealthy and influential men.

These officials became in many cases confidants and favourites of the king and wielded political influence.[8]

But that also meant that potentially they could be dangerous if their sympathies were won by the king's enemies. We are told that these two men are in jail for crimes against Pharaoh himself. Perhaps the Pharaoh thought they were out to get him.

We are meant to feel a cranking-up of the tension in the story as Moses tells it. Here is our man Joseph not only in jail with these high-ranking criminals, but even dancing attendance on those who had attended the Pharaoh himself. What Joseph couldn't know was that his encounter with these men was going to lead to his elevation out of the prison and up to the top of the political career tree. However, that lies in the future, and Joseph has no idea of what is going to happen. One thing we do know is that the king's decision, taken in the normal course of events within his royal palace, unfolded according to the providence of God.

With God in the depths

Many of us have had periods in life when we have felt as if we were in the pit! Life today in the West is very highly

---

[7] Genesis 37:2; 41:46

[8] K. A. Kitchen quoted in Waltke, *Genesis*, 525

charged. The race goes to the strong and the weak go to the wall. Being someone with integrity is no guarantee of recognition or appreciation. In fact people take every opportunity to attack those who have moral principles and in particular those with Christian values. As I write this, I have just read an article in which a respected journalist in the UK has attacked Christianity and argued that its presence has a detrimental effect on society:

> *Religious belief can cause damage to a society, contributing towards high murder rates, abortion, sexual promiscuity and suicide, according to research published today. According to the study, belief in and worship of God are not only unnecessary for a healthy society but may actually contribute to social problems.*[9]

This article delighted to skew the information in a way that attacked Christian believers. Referring to a study of the US, it argued that there were higher rates of homicide, juvenile and early adult mortality, sexually transmitted disease, teen pregnancy and abortion in that church-going democracy than in other more secular societies. This sort of article is designed to make us question whether it is worth taking a stand for the things of God. Is it worth the misrepresentation and misunderstanding that goes with loyalty to God in a secular world? Do you really believe that 'in all things God works for the good of those who love him'?[10] This is part of what we mean when we affirm the orthodox Christian faith that God is 'almighty'. We affirm that God is both good and all powerful.

Apparently some find this teaching difficult to take.

---

[9] September 27, 2005 *The Times,* Societies worse off 'when they have God on their side' By Ruth Gledhill, Religion Correspondent

Tony Campolo, a popular speaker on the conference circuit, suggests that the Old Testament never asserts the omnipotence of God, that is, that God is almighty. So, for instance, he says that we should not suggest that God could have prevented Hurricane Katrina from devastating the Gulf Coast. Raising the question, 'Why didn't God do something?' Campolo writes:

> *Unfortunately, there are a lot of bad answers. One such answer is that somehow all suffering is a part of God's great plan. In the midst of agonies, someone is likely to quote from the Bible, telling us that if we would just be patient, we eventually would see 'all things work together for the good, for those who love God, and are called according to His purposes' (Rom. 8:28).*

I don't doubt that God can bring good out of tragedies, but the Bible is clear that God is not the author of evil! (James 1:15) Statements like that dishonour God, and are responsible for driving more people away from Christianity than all the arguments that atheistic philosophers could ever muster. When the floods swept into the Gulf Coast, God was the first one who wept. [11]

Campolo is clearly right when he reminds us that God is not the author of evil. The Bible always affirms that. He is also right to warn us against rushing to explain to people why this or that tragedy may have happened. That can be totally insensitive. We simply do not see as God sees. But what he says next is wrong:

> *Perhaps we would do well to listen to the likes of Rabbi Harold Kushner, who contends that God is not really as powerful as we*

[10] Romans 8:28

[11] Tony Campolo, www.beliefnet.com/story/174/story_17423.html

have claimed. Nowhere in the Hebrew Scriptures does it say that God is omnipotent. Kushner points out that omnipotence is a Greek philosophical concept, but it is not in his Bible. Instead, the Hebrew Bible contends that God is mighty. That means that God is a greater force in the universe than all the other forces combined.

Rabbi Harold Kushner does indeed deny the omnipotence of God. Indeed, he suggests that we should simply understand that God is doing the best He can do under the circumstances. This is his rather fatalistic response to the Holocaust. But it is no Christian response to say that when things go wrong we should comfort ourselves with the thought that God couldn't stop that thing happening. That is a counsel of despair and it is contrary to the Bible's plain teaching.

The *Westminster Shorter Catechism* puts it like this:

Q.11 What are God's works of providence?
A. God's works of providence are His most holy, wise and powerful preserving and governing all His creatures and all their actions.

The word 'omnipotence' may not appear in the Bible, but the teaching that He is almighty is to be found everywhere. Our lives are not at the mercy of nature nor are we the victims of circumstances, but our lives are in the hands of God.

God Himself is the main actor in the Joseph drama. Everything is happening according to His master plan. Ultimately the closing of the prison doors is designed by the Lord to open palace doors, but only in His timing.[12]

---

[12] Acts 7:10

The story of Joseph and the message of the Bible is that Abraham's God is not limited to doing the best He can. Joseph may be in the jail, but 'the LORD was with him', and He is setting him up for the great future that lies ahead of him. All the time and through all the details, God is establishing His purpose and working out His will, through and in spite of people's actions.

There is an interesting indicator that God was with Joseph. These two important men, Pharaoh's cupbearer and baker, are thrown into prison for having done something to offend the king, and Joseph is allocated to attend them. By whom? By the prison warden? No! By the captain of the bodyguard![13] His identity has already been revealed earlier in the story; his name is Potiphar.[14] This man has apparently softened towards Joseph, perhaps having realized that he might have been wrong about him. In any event, it is a little blessing for Joseph at an important time.

The dream-maker

The three pairs of dreams – to Joseph (37:5-11), to the butler and baker (40:1-11), and to Pharaoh (41:1-40) – show a God who sovereignly controls destiny. Here is knowledge that lies outside of imperial power.[15]

It was a common thing in the Egypt of this time to take dreams seriously. People believed them to be a medium through which the gods communicated with humans about the future, and in fact people were paid well to interpret dreams. The popular belief was (as we saw with Joseph's dreams earlier) that when dreams came in twos, they were to be taken seriously.

---

[13] Genesis 40:3-4
[14] Genesis 39:1
[15] Waltke, *Genesis*, 526

One night both the cupbearer and the baker of the king of Egypt, who were both confined in the prison, dreamed vividly. Each had his own dream, and each dream was such that each man felt he needed to have it interpreted [16] Once again we see the hand of God in these events. Here are two men, being attended to by Joseph, and God gives to each of them a dream on the same night! Because they are in jail they have no access to the professional people whose job it was to explain dreams, so they are dejected and down because they sense in their superstition that there is something special about these dreams. God takes the very religious background of these men and makes it serve His purpose. This is Joseph's cue, and he steps up boldly and takes on his role as God's spokesman.

Joseph gives God glory

It's clear that once again Joseph is keen to give God the glory. When he was confronted with the temptation to sleep with his boss's wife, he resisted not only out of personal integrity and loyalty to his boss, but above all out of loyalty to God. Here he immediately makes it clear that he does not have any independent ability to interpret these dreams apart from God's gift and help. He is giving God glory:

> And Joseph said to them, 'Do not interpretations belong to God?'[17]

The meaning is not given because of superior wisdom or as a result of magical incantations. God gives the knowledge

---

[16] Genesis 40:5
[17] Genesis 40:8

to whoever he pleases. Notice that Joseph doesn't use the covenant name LORD when speaking to the Egyptians, but the universal title 'God'. Israel's Jahweh is not only their covenant partner, but He is their God too, since He is God of the whole world. Joseph's humility is very evident here, but so is his faith; 'Please tell them to me,' he asks. He accepts his prophetic role, believing himself to be chosen by God for this very thing. He is conscious that God rules over the affairs of men.

God still gives gifts to people today. They may be different from Joseph's gifts, but the purpose of them is still to give God glory. He gives us gifts of speech or hospitality or service in order to be of use to Him and to other people. We should be humble in our exercise of them. We should learn from Joseph to have a God-centred focus in our lives, able to discern when God is opening a door of opportunity for us to serve Him, even if taking that opportunity involves a step of faith and dependence upon God, as it did for Joseph in this instance. He had to believe that God would reveal the meaning of these dreams to him. If that did not happen, Joseph would look very foolish!

Declaring God's word
In response to Joseph's offer, the first man tells Joseph his dream:

> *So the chief cupbearer told his dream to Joseph and said to him, 'In my dream there was a vine before me, and on the vine there were three branches. As soon as it budded, its blossoms shot forth, and the clusters ripened into grapes. Pharaoh's cup was in my hand, and I took the grapes and pressed them into Pharaoh's cup and placed the cup in Pharaoh's hand.'[18]*

---

[18] Genesis 40:9-11

He gets a great answer:

> *'In three days Pharaoh will lift up your head and restore you to your office, and you shall place Pharaoh's cup in his hand as formerly, when you were his cupbearer.'*[19]

The second man, Pharaoh's baker, is listening in. He seems to show signs of being reluctant to tell his dream, but he's encouraged by what he hears of the interpretation for the cupbearer, so he too tells his dream:

> *When the chief baker saw that the interpretation was favourable, he said to Joseph, "I also had a dream: there were three cake baskets on my head, and in the uppermost basket there were all sorts of baked food for Pharaoh, but the birds were eating it out of the basket on my head."*[20]

Did he expect the same outcome? It's not hard to imagine him hanging on every word, and to begin with the interpretation does sound promising. Joseph begins with exactly the same words, 'In three days Pharaoh will lift up your head,' which was often a way of expressing the idea that someone was going to be exalted, but he doesn't stop there:

> *'In three days Pharaoh will lift up your head—from you!—and hang you on a tree. And the birds will eat the flesh from you.'*[21]

Joseph listens to the dreams and gives the interpretations. What is he doing? He is declaring that God rules in heaven

---

[19] Genesis 40:12-13
[20] Genesis 40:16-17
[21] Genesis 40:19

and on earth. He becomes God's spokesman and he passes on God's Word, which is a message of both life and death. It is a message of life for one man and death for the other. God's Word always has this double-edged quality.[22] It is both good and bad news simultaneously. He speaks of the future too, of God's purpose to resolve the ultimate issues of this life.

In all this Joseph reminds us of our Lord Jesus. He constantly spoke God's Word to His generation. He witnessed to the truth of God and spoke about the judgment to come. He too spoke of the respective destinies of men and women, both good and bad. He told the truth, which is not always easy to take! Isn't it true that often we are tempted to soft-pedal the message of God for our day? We want to be positive in what we say, so we find ways of getting round some of the hard sayings of the Bible. We want a God who is only love and never threatens the wicked. We want to be able to tell people that there are many ways to God rather than declare that there is only one Saviour for the whole world. And there are many people in the world, false teachers, who tell others exactly what they want to hear. They know exactly what plays well in the wine bars and media circles in which they move, and they refashion the Bible's message to suit their audience. Jeremiah spoke out against such people in his day:

> *from prophet to priest, everyone deals falsely. They have healed the wound of my people lightly, saying, 'Peace, peace', when there is no peace.*[23]

---

[22] Hebrews 4:12
[23] Jeremiah 6:14

Joseph witnesses to the right of God to do as He pleases in His world. Listen to these words by George Lawson:

> *Let us remember that divine providence is under no obligation to be equally kind to us all. And that prosperity and adversity, life and death, are distributed to men by One who has the right to do what he will with his own.*[24]

These dreams raise the issue of how God communicates to us today. In the Bible we find God communicating by *acts of power* — in creation, the Flood and in the exodus from Egypt. He also communicated by *words of revelation*. For example, He spoke through Moses, giving him the first five books of the Bible. He also spoke through prophets to whom He gave a special message. Sometimes God revealed Himself through *visions,* as He did with Jacob. In those cases people actually saw heavenly realities and heard heavenly messages. He also spoke through *dreams*, sometimes through people who had no connection with the nation of Israel. The features of these dreams are usually in need of interpretation. Joseph and Daniel are Old Testament examples of this. In the New Testament there are strictly speaking only six dreams, which are all recorded in the book of Matthew. Now all of these took place as part of God's revelation to us which has now been completed and collected in our Holy Scriptures. The definitive answer to the question, 'Does God speak to us through dreams today?' is found in Hebrews 1:1-2:

> *Long ago, at many times and in many ways, God spoke to our fathers by the prophets, but in these last days he has spoken to us by his Son, whom he appointed the heir of all things, through whom also he created the world.*

---

[24] George Lawson, *The History of Joseph*, 163

The author is pointing out that the fullness of revelation is now complete and final in the coming of Jesus Christ. God's greatest revelation has come in His Son.[25] The Spirit reveals the Son and all truth through the apostles, as Jesus taught.[26] No further revelation is needed. He is God's final word. As F. F. Bruce points out:

> *The story of divine revelation is a story of progression up to Christ, but there is no progression beyond him.*[27]

The Bible is not being written today, it is complete and it is sufficient. So we do not see the variety of means of revelation that we saw while it was being compiled. We have it in our hands, in the pages of the book that the Holy Spirit inspired and preserved to teach and direct God's church in every age. This is not to deny that God can use dreams to unsettle us, to apply His Word directly to us, to arouse someone to search for Jesus as happens among Muslims in some closed societies. But these offer no new revelation; they are part of God's amazing way of using our regular human activity to work where the normal means of grace are not available.

God's sustaining grace

That Joseph's faith remains strong is clear from his response to the cupbearer, 'remember me.'[28] Even after his reputation as an interpreter of dreams has been established by the precise fulfilment of his interpretations, Joseph has to languish in jail for two more years. God's timetable is

---

[25] Colossians 1:15-23
[26] John 16:13-14
[27] Bruce quoted in Currid, *Genesis*, Vol.2, 240
[28] Genesis 40:14

not always ours. All in all it takes thirteen years in slavery and prison before Joseph is elevated to the position he was destined for. From his perspective, he at no time had any guarantee of this happening. Indeed, it is improbable that he would ever have imagined such a sequence of events, not even in his wildest dreams! From God's perspective, however, it was always sure.

Nowhere in the text does it say that Joseph gets discouraged or despairs. In spite of being hardworking and faithful in his witness, in spite of giving God the glory in the interpretation of the two men's dreams, he has to languish in this jail for another two years until he is thirty years of age. It may seem surprising that there is no mention at all of his emotional life up to this point in the text, though later Moses describes how he pours out his grief and weeps copious tears when he is reunited with his brothers.[29] That fact tells us that Joseph had a rich emotional life; he was no hard man, and he felt deeply.

The Bible is quick to tell us of the feelings of others in Scripture. The book of Psalms is full of honest, even heart-rending outpourings of anger, grief, disillusionment, bafflement, self-pity, anguish, and questioning. That book is in the Bible to say to believers that we can say anything to God, we can come as we are and say what we need to say, we can 'cast all our burdens' on the Lord. It is not a mark of weakness, or of unbelief. In fact, on the contrary, to express doubt and difficulty to God is a mark of faith! You have to believe in Him to complain to Him. There is nothing but tender reassurance in the Bible for those whose hearts are wrung with pain, loneliness and regret.

---

[29] Genesis 43:30, 45:2

And there is nothing but comfort for those who suffer, whether mentally or physically. To say otherwise or to suggest that people who call out in such a way are faltering in faith or obedience is both cruel and misguided. Even our Lord Jesus cried out in anguish in the garden and on the cross. It is part of our humanity and it is part of living in a world that is out of joint. We can't speculate about Joseph, but we can say this, God sustained Him. He always does.

This chapter ends with the words, 'Yet the cupbearer did not remember Joseph, but forgot him.' People often let us down, don't they? They make great promises to call us, to visit us, to marry us, to love us, to provide for us, to be there for us, to back us, to support us, to promote us, to give us a rise … the list is endless. We humans are not good at keeping our promises. Even where we are well-meaning, we have a habit of dying on one another and so we experience the ultimate desertion. But we know the end of this story. We know that God did not forget Joseph. When our Lord was buried in the tomb, people may well have thought, 'That's it then!' Certainly Jesus' disciples did. Certainly those disciples plodding down the Emmaus road did when they told their unrecognised fellow-traveller, 'we thought that this was the one who would deliver Israel!'[30]

God had not forgotten Joseph. He had not forgotten his covenant promises to Abraham. He had planned to save many people. He had planned to stop the covenant family's absorption into the Canaanite way of life. He had plans to preserve the seed, the family tree of the Messiah himself, the Saviour of the world. Those plans required that Joseph stay in prison so that he could one day be exalted to Pharaoh's

---

[30] Luke 24:21

side. So he stays there until God's good time arrives. Joseph still hoped in God, but it was hope deferred. So if you feel as if God has forgotten about you and your needs, don't give up. Sometimes God's purposes don't go in a straight line, but they always arrive at at His intended destination.

6
'Uneasy lies the head'

J. K. Rowling first thought of Harry Potter whilst travelling in a train back in 1990. 'Harry just strolled into my head fully formed,' she said. She worked on the book for several years, finding quiet moments while her daughter napped. Several publishers turned down the finished manuscript before one took an interest. The rest, they say, is history. Her sixth title, *Harry Potter and the Half-Blood Prince*, set a new world record for a first printing, with 10.8 million copies hitting stores on July 16, 2005, the first day of its general release. *Harry Potter and the Deathly Hallows*, J.K. Rowling's seventh and final book in the Harry Potter series, has broken all publishing records in the US, selling a record 8.3 million copies in the first 24 hours.[1] The Harry Potter books are now available in 65 languages and have sold more than 325 million copies across the globe.[2]

---

[1] Scholastic, Ms Rowling's US publishers
[2] As of July 2007

We love to hear a good 'rags to riches' story. We are fascinated to hear how people have risen out of obscurity to fame and from poverty to great wealth. It is the plot-line of some of the best in fairy tales and of the most compelling fiction. When it happens in real life, as it did to J.K. Rowling, it is quite amazing!

On the sidelines
The first part of chapter 41 tells the 'rags to riches' story of the day when Joseph is transferred from the pit to the palace and transformed from prisoner into prime minister. Of course there is more to it than that, but his rise to the top is unquestionably meteoric. The previous episodes in his story have been preparing us for this outcome. There have been indications that God was with His man in the difficult experiences he'd gone through at home, in the house of Potiphar his master and in the palace prison.

This scene in the drama begins with Joseph on the sidelines. It is now exactly two years since the events of the previous chapter, and the king's birthday has rolled around again. When Joseph had interpreted the dreams of his two fellow prisoners, he had given one of the men the good news that he would be restored to his position as cupbearer to the king, and this had come to pass. For the other man, Joseph had been the bringer of the bad news that he would be hanged, and that word too had come true. In telling the interpretation of the dream, he had urged the cupbearer to remember him when eventually he was elevated to his former place in the palace:

> 'only remember me, when it is well with you, and please do me this kindness to mention me to Pharaoh.'[3]

---

[3] Genesis 40:14

But the man had forgotten: 'the chief cupbearer did not remember Joseph, but forgot him.'[4]

That is where things stand as this scene opens. Again the same old questions come to mind, questions believers regularly ask whenever things don't go according to plan. Has Joseph been abandoned completely? Has God forgotten him? Joseph undoubtedly trusts in God, but he is unaware of what is going on beyond his prison cell. Of course we know the real answer, which is that his imprisonment is part of God's plan to elevate him one day. As one hymn writer put it,

> *Thrice bless'd is he to whom is given*
> *The instinct that can tell*
> *That God is on the field when he*
> *Is most invisible.*[5]

The Dream-maker

While Joseph is on the sidelines, somewhere in the palace not too far away the king is thrown into dismay by a dream.

Dreams can be disturbing and disorienting. In the *Voyage of the Dawn Treader*, C.S. Lewis describes an island where dreams come true:

> 'This is the island I've been looking for this long time', said one of the sailors. 'Fools', said a man from the island, stamping his foot with rage. 'That's the sort of talk that brought me here, and I'd better have been drowned or never born'. Suddenly every man began rowing as they never had before, 'for it had taken them just that half minute to remember certain dreams they had had – dreams that make you afraid to sleep again'.

---

[4] Genesis 40:23
[5] Frederick William Faber, 'The Right Must Win'

Most of our dreams are reflections of our subconscious fears or desires. My wife regularly tells me her dreams, but I remember mine only rarely. The only dream I ever remember is a repeated dream of falling from a tall building. It probably reflects my fear of heights!

Pharaoh's dream on this occasion is not one of that type. It is given to him by God Himself. These dreams put the most powerful man on earth in the same boat as his two servants, the cupbearer and the baker, who had been in jail with Joseph two years before. Kings may be powerful, but they can be as uneasy at night as anyone else. 'Uneasy lies the head that wears the crown,' wrote Shakespeare.[6]

It shouldn't surprise us that God is able to unsettle such a great man in this way. Proverbs 21:1 says:

> *The king's heart is a stream of water in the hand of the LORD; he turns it wherever he will.*

God is never stuck when it comes to implementing His will in the world. It must have seemed impossible to Joseph that he should ever get an audience with the greatest monarch in the world, ruler of the only superpower of that time. Yet God cuts through all the machinery of government, all the layers of bureaucracy and all the systems of communication and gets the king's attention at his most vulnerable moment, in the middle of the night! Knowing that God has our destiny in His hands is a source of great peace and comfort to us who are believers. It is when we take matters into our own hands that we often make a mess of things. When we try to manipulate circumstances to achieve our ends,

---

[6] William Shakespeare, *Henry IV Part II* Act 3

even when they are good ends, we invariably make things worse.

The river Nile provides the backdrop to the Pharaoh's dreams. In Egyptian mythology, the Nile was personified in Hapi, the Egyptians' number-one god. They regarded Egypt itself as the gift of the Nile, and looked to it for fertility and, indeed, for life itself. The nation's existence was completely dependent on it. In the thinking of Pharaoh, it was the Nile god Hapi who sustained Egypt and provided for her. So these dreams were full of significance for the ruler of all Egypt.

In his first dream, Pharaoh saw two groups of seven cows. The first group were 'attractive and plump,' they were healthy, sturdy and strong, 'and they fed in the reed grass.'[7] The second group were 'ugly and thin,' and 'the ugly, thin cows ate up the seven attractive, plump cows.'[8] What was he to make of it? He went back to sleep and started to dream again. This time he dreamt about seven ears of corn which were 'plump and good', but then they too were swallowed up by seven ears that were 'thin and blighted'.[9] Not surprisingly, the Pharaoh woke up in some distress, so he sent for all the magicians and wise men of Egypt.

In those days many nations had drifted so far away from the true God that they had turned to magic to manipulate events for their own benefit, and that was particularly true of Egypt This ancient Egyptian practice has a modern counterpart in the New Age ideas and astrological interest we see around us in our sophisticated Western society. Then

---

[7] Genesis 41:2
[8] Genesis 41:4
[9] Genesis 41:5-7

as now, however, the magicians can provide no answers. It is only the Creator who can give meaning and purpose to life and change the course of events.

So Pharaoh calls in the pagan priests, the magicians and the wise men of Egypt to see if they can offer an explanation. He tells them his dreams, but not one of these wise men can interpret them for him.[10] Magicians and wise men reappear in the Bible story several hundred years later when Moses turns up in the Pharaoh's court and demands in God's name that the Israelites should be allowed to leave Egypt.[11] They represent the best that pagan religion can do. They stand for the wisdom of this present world. Yet they are useless when it really counts. All this heightens the tension in the story and leaves room for God to get all the glory. Both of these incidents involving magicians and wise men in the Bible stories have at their heart the question, 'Which god is God?'

Total recall

It is at this point that the cupbearer remembers Joseph ... at last! Something in the similarity of the circumstances jogs his memory. He is convicted about having forgotten Joseph's request.[12] He uses a word meaning 'offences', which highlights his realisation that he has wronged both Pharaoh and Joseph. When he sees the distress of the king, he remembers his own. He uses language that drives home to the Pharaoh how similar his experience was to the king's:

---

[10] Genesis 41:8
[11] Exodus 6: 10-13
[12] Genesis 41:9

> '*A young Hebrew was there with us, a servant of the captain of the guard. When we told him, he interpreted our dreams to us, giving an interpretation to each man according to his dream. And as he interpreted to us, so it came about. I was restored to my office, and the baker was hanged.*'[13]

These words of an eyewitness prepare Pharaoh to accept Joseph's interpretation as God's ordained word.

This is what the Holy Spirit does in people's hearts still. He provides an inner conviction that the word is true. John Calvin puts it like this:

> *The testimony of the Spirit is more excellent than all reason [that is, human reason only gets us so far]. For just as God alone is a fit witness of himself in his word, so also that word will not find acceptance in men's hearts before it is sealed by the inward testimony of the Spirit. The same Spirit, therefore, who has spoken through the mouths of the prophets must penetrate into our hearts to persuade us that they faithfully proclaimed what had been divinely commanded.*[14]

We need the Spirit who inspired the Scripture to open our eyes and train our minds to understand and open our hearts so that we are willing to receive God's Word for what it is.

This is what is happening in the heart of the cupbearer. He realises that God was in the interpretation he was given. As Christians, we do not normally have dreams which communicate God's will to us today. His word normally comes through the Bible – God's Word written - but the

---

[14] John Calvin, *Institutes of the Christian Religion*, trans. F. L. Battles (The Library of Christian Classics 20; Philadelphia: Westminster Press, 1960), 1.7.4. p79

Spirit gives the same witness in our hearts that the word is of God and can be trusted.

Pharaoh's reaction to the cupbearer's confession produces a flurry of activity.[15] The staccato like repetition of a series of verbs in just one verse emphasises the speed with which the whole drama moves along. Joseph's feet hardly touch the ground as he is whisked (it says he was 'run out') out of the prison (literally 'the pit') to appear before the king. He shaves himself and changes his clothes in preparation for meeting the king, so that by the time he appears before Pharaoh he looks like an Egyptian. Once again clothes are important (remember his famous coat?), as he is given new clothes to wear to make him ready to see the king.

The king uses all kinds of words to flatter Joseph. He need only have commanded Joseph to interpret his dream, but he is desperate to get an answer to this problem:

'I have heard it said of you that when you hear a dream you can interpret it.'[16]

What a temptation for Joseph to keep quiet and take the credit! But he can't do it. Joseph is very strong in his answer. 'It is not me!' are his first words. Actually his language is explosive; there is only one word in the Hebrew. He will not take any credit to himself. He is not a magician or a professional dream-interpreter. His ability comes totally from God:

'God will give Pharaoh a favourable answer.'[17]

---

[15] Genesis 41:14
[16] Genesis 41:15
[17] Genesis 41:16

It might have been easy for him at this point to allow the king to think he was really so talented. After all, here he was in the presence of the greatest man on earth all dressed up in royal clothes! Could this be his opportunity? But Joseph gave credit and glory to God.

One Sunday morning Charles Spurgeon was greeted by members of his congregation. One man said to him, 'Sir that was the greatest sermon I have ever heard and that you have ever preached!' Spurgeon turned to him and said, 'Yes, the devil told me that ten minutes ago.'[18] We do well to remember that all our gifts and graces come from God and that He will not share His glory with another.

The Interpreter
Throughout his interpretation, Joseph emphasises God's central role. He makes it clear that God will give Pharaoh the answer that will bring him peace.[19] Both the dreams and the interpretation are from God,[20] and are concerned with what God is about to do.[21]

Joseph tells Pharaoh that the two dreams belong together. The dreams used two symbols to represent the same two things. The seven cows and the seven stalks of corn each symbolised periods of seven years. The fat cows and healthy corn represented seven years of abundance, whilst the thin cows and poor stalks of corn represented seven years of famine which would devour all the benefits of the previous good years. Joseph stresses that God has been good to show the king what He is going to do.

---

[18] Currid, *Genesis*, 259
[19] Genesis 41:16
[20] Genesis 41:25
[21] Genesis 41:28

'God has shown Pharaoh what he is about to do.'[22]

There is a clear contrast between the helplessness of the most powerful man on earth and the one and only true God, who is going to have His way in Egypt.

'The thing is fixed by God, and God will shortly bring it about.'[23]

From the start, Joseph is God-centred in what he says to Pharaoh.

Pharaoh feels unsettled by these dreams, and so he should; they are a reminder of his impotence to influence events of nature. This episode is a helpful reminder to us that leaders, politicians and even dictators are not the ones who make history. History is in God's hands. He raises up and then disposes of them as He pleases. Some time ago, I read in the press of a discussion in Russia about the future of the rotting mummy of Lenin in the mausoleum in Red Square. 'It isn't doing too well,' said the New York Times, 'sprouting grass from time to time!' This is where all the great men of the world are going, even when they try to immortalise themselves.

Joseph's next words are a bold move. He is aware that knowing what the dreams mean is not enough, and is prepared to take the risk of giving some advice. God's sovereignty does not negate human responsibility, so the king needs to do something with this knowledge.

The fact that God has determined the matter, that God hastens to bring it to pass, is precisely the reason for responsible leaders to take measures![24]

---

[22] Genesis 41:28 NIV

[23] Genesis 41:32

[24] von Rad, *Genesis*, 376, cited in Waltke, *Genesis*, 536

Joseph spells out the action that needs to be taken. This particular event, the impending famine, is not a judgment, rather 'it is one of life's irregularities.'[25] But it will happen very quickly, so time is of the essence. He urges the king to appoint a vizier, a wise and influential man to oversee the planning and operation of the measures he's about to outline. He is wise enough to stress the king's authority and not to promote himself.[26] At each point, Joseph stresses that such a person would be answerable to the king.[27] Joseph demonstrates great wisdom in the way he conducts himself, and what he was advising was not without precedent. We know from the Egyptian records that from time to time a vizier was appointed in Egypt as a kind of prime minister, or else as a minister of state with a particular department under him. Very probably Joseph would have been aware of this from his years living in Egypt in Potiphar's household. The fact that this strategy was a tried and tested one in Egypt helps to verify the biblical record of events.

The plan Joseph outlines is to organise a way of storing grain during the good years, so that when the famine comes there is more than enough set aside to feed the people during those years. Here is public power used for the public good.[28] Those who can pay will pay, and those who cannot will be helped out. It is a very enlightened policy! Also, Joseph stresses that the hand of God is in all this. All of our lives are lived under God's eye and in His hands.

This is the doctrine of the Providence of God. It is a source of the most enormous comfort to the believer to

---

[25] Derek Kidner, *Genesis*, 196

[26] Genesis 41:33

[27] Genesis 41:35

[28] Brueggemann, *Genesis*, 295-96

know that God rules in His world, and to know where history is headed. That is why we are so committed to getting the gospel to the world. It is Christ's kingdom that is growing and our task is to take the message to the nations, 'and then the end will come.'[29] For God rules at two levels. First, He rules universally. So here He exercises His power for the preservation of people in Egypt and elsewhere, even though they do not recognise his rule. Secondly, He also rules over His people. Here in the story of Joseph, God works at one level (in his universal rule) so as to preserve his people (what is known as His mediatorial rule). As God's people, we benefit from much that God does in His universal reign over the world, but ultimately the only hope for the world is through what God is doing in the church as we hold out the word of life.

Straight to the top

As this scene ends, we find Joseph reaching the summit of earthly power and influence.

Then Pharaoh said to Joseph, 'Since God has shown you all this, there is none so discerning and wise as you are. You shall be over my house, and all my people shall order themselves as you command. Only as regards the throne will I be greater than you.'[30]

This is such an amazing turnaround. Joseph was in jail in the morning and by evening he is sitting beside the Pharaoh as his second-in-command over all Egypt which, like the US today, was the greatest world power of that time.

It is interesting to notice how the king acknowledges that

---

[29] Matthew 24:14
[30] Genesis 41:39-40
[31] Genesis 41:38

the 'Spirit of God' rests on Joseph.[31] Pharaoh would not have understood this in the way we would, but he spoke more than he knew when he said to his servants, 'Can we find a man like this, in whom is the Spirit of God?' What this pagan monarch is recognising, is that the power of God is with this man. In the Old Testament, the Spirit of God gives people extraordinary wisdom to lead, to build the tabernacle, to prophesy, to show discernment, to interpret dreams and to plot an effective course of action. Here the Spirit gives the king faith to believe what he could not empirically verify beforehand. It is hard to credit how astonishing Pharaoh's reaction is, because not only does he accept the interpretation as true, but he makes the leap of deciding that Joseph the interpreter would be the best man to do the job. Only the supernatural work of the spirit could do that. Centuries later, another pagan king recognised the hand of God upon a foreigner in his court. The Babylonian king Belshazzar described Daniel in these terms:

"I have heard that the spirit of the gods is in you and that you have insight, intelligence and outstanding wisdom."[32]

Joseph is invested with enormous power and influence. A formal investiture event is described.[33] He is given all the visible trappings of power and prestige. He is given the Egyptian equivalent of a limo (the second chariot – much like the vice-presidential limo!) in which to travel round the kingdom. The 'golden necklace' is also a sign of high honour. He's given the king's signet ring, which was the same as having the king's credit card, so that whenever he produced

---

[32] Daniel 5:14
[33] Genesis 41:41

it, he would get what he wanted. Joseph is now to perform the same functions as the king himself, and everyone has to do what Joseph tells them As he goes around, people are to bow before him out of respect for his office. He had once dreamed that his brothers and his father would bow before him, but now all Egypt will bow the knee before him.[34] He is even given a new name, Zaphenath-paneah, which means, '*God has spoken and he lives.*' Imagine! This new Egyptian name is itself a testimony to Joseph's God – 'He speaks and lives!' Yet Joseph also finds himself married to an Egyptian wife. So he gets an Egyptian name and even a wife! He is married into one of the most powerful families in all Egypt, that of the priest of On,[35] and On was a city at the centre of sun-worship. Might this have been an attempt to unite the power of two mighty gods? In all probability, Joseph wouldn't have had any choice in this regard. The wife came with the job!

Joseph is now very well connected. This was a great opportunity but also a great temptation. The question is this: how will Joseph do once he's rich and famous? Will he become Egyptianised? Will he forget his responsibility to the God of his fathers? Will he simply settle down and luxuriate in the life of the court? Will the one who has been faithful in adversity be knocked out of the race by fame, influence or wealth?

The truth is that as Christians we soon buckle under the weight of the temptation to love the things of this world. No sooner do we start to earn a bit more and begin to mix with the influential, or the rich and famous, than we lose our edge. We make a hundred little compromises that erode our faith and throttle our devotion. It is always a challenge

---

[34] Genesis 41:42-4
[35] Genesis 41:45

to the influential and wealthy to remember they are called to be humble servants of King Jesus. When you are a servant of the living God living in an alien land, as we Christians are, how far do you go in accommodating to the culture? This question has always vexed believers down through the centuries. Often we have got it wrong. We have withdrawn from the society we live in; we have retreated into our ecclesiastical ghettos; we have lost touch with the world. At other times we have sold out. In the interests of evangelism or perhaps relevance; under pressure from the authorities or simply under peer pressure; with the best motives in the world or the worst, we have let the world dictate how the church should be and how the Christian should behave. The problem today tends to be the latter rather than the former.

Here is Joseph and he goes pretty far in the world's direction. He accepts a new Egyptian name, much as Daniel was to do in Babylon centuries later. He has an unbelieving wife and works for a regime with values and beliefs totally at odds with his own. But although both Joseph and Daniel accepted pagan names and worked within the governing system of the day for the good of the societies they lived in, they drew the line at accepting pagan religion. They had the discernment to see the difference.

Giving God glory

Joseph serves God in the courts of Pharaoh with the same devotion as he served God in slavery and in prison. Joseph had come to Egypt when he was seventeen,[36] and he is now thirty.[37] He has waited a long time for life to get a bit easier, yet he doesn't sit back and revel in the new wealth

---

[36] Genesis 37:2
[37] Genesis 41:46

and luxurious lifestyle that is now available to him. He gets on with the job he's been given of accumulating grain for the years of famine to come. He also has children. He gives them names that are a testimony to his faith: *'God has made me forget my trouble'* and *'God has made me fruitful.'*[38] We mustn't miss the fact that this man declares his allegiance by giving his children Hebrew names. He had been given an Egyptian name and his wife's name is Asenath, which means, *'she who belongs to the goddess Neit,'* but the names given to these young men who are destined to spend their days among the Nile elite are Hebrew ones, as a testimony to Joseph's clear stand for the things of God.

To visit Joseph and meet his family was to be reminded that here was a man who was keenly aware of God's providence in his life. He lived in the presence of God. He could say with the Psalmist, 'Yet I am always with you, you hold me by my right hand.'[39] I remember my father holding my hand as we walked along the street when I was very young. It was my security and I loved holding his hand. Here the Psalmist is thinking about God holding his hand, and it is this same sense of God overseeing his life that gave Joseph perspective and sustained him.

Joseph was in Egypt, but he was not an Egyptian. He did not lose his identity as one of God's people. He was in the world but not of it. He gave God glory in the hardest place of all. That wasn't the pit or the prison, but the palace. It is very often harder for a person to maintain their love for God in prosperity than in adversity. He believed God. He was the only person in Egypt at that time who trusted in God, as far as we know. It was Joseph against the world. Yet

---

[38] Genesis 41:51-2
[39] Psalm 73:23

he worked as hard in this top position as he had when out of the eye of the public. Sometimes, when people get more money or more free time, they become lazy in their work for God. They lose sight of the need to sacrifice time and money for His kingdom. When people are given positions of influence, even in church, it sometimes goes to their head and they want to be treated differently from everyone else. They forget that God was the one who brought them to that position and that He is the one to be honoured and obeyed.

A blessing to the nations

This chapter ends with the nations coming to Egypt for bread.

> *All the earth came to Egypt to Joseph to buy grain, because the famine was severe over all the earth.*[40]

The salvation of the world depends on this one descendant of the patriarchs. At one level here is something of a fulfilment of the promise to Abraham, 'through you all the families of earth will be blessed.'[41] What we have here is a partial fulfilment of that, but it is also a pointer to the fullest form of its fulfilment in Jesus Christ.

We have seen that Joseph often appears to have a career similar to that of our Lord Jesus. We have seen him sold for twenty pieces of silver; our Lord was sold for thirty. Now, at age 30, he begins his life work, as our Lord did at the same age. God took Joseph from the pit to the palace, and our Lord was raised from the cross and the grave to his throne of glory. God's wisdom far outstrips the wisdom of this world.

---

[40] Genesis 41:57
[41] Genesis 12:3

Here in Joseph's exaltation we see a glimpse of the success that accompanies Jesus in his exaltation to his Father's throne. From that throne, He dispenses blessings to the world. People come to Jesus from all over the world and He gives them the blessings of salvation. And just as all were commanded to bow down before Joseph, so God has 'highly exalted him and given him a name that is above every name, that at the name of Jesus every knee shall bow and every tongue confess that he is LORD to the glory of God the Father.'[42]

Genesis chapter 41 reaches its climax with Joseph identified as the saviour of the world at that time of famine. People from every nation that is in need of bread come to Egypt and buy it from Joseph. Jesus said:

> *'I am the bread of life. He who comes to me will never go hungry.'*[43]

He still invites people to come to him to find their soul hunger satisfied. Where I live in London, we are surrounded by people who think they have everything. Their self-worth can be gauged by their net worth. Yet the best kind of pleasure they can come up with is to go out on a Saturday night and get smashed! I read in the newspapers about one man who blew a million pounds on a drinks party. Can you believe that? What has gone wrong? Can their money not buy them something a bit better than that? What of us? Are you experiencing a famine of the soul? Then come to Jesus who wants to satisfy you, to feed you, to lavish His kindness on you for free. He invites us to come with our emptiness, so that He can fill us.

---

[42] Philippians 2:9-11
[43] John 6:35

7

A Severe Mercy

How far will God go to bring a family to Himself? Apparently He will go as far as it takes! In chapter 42 we find Him working through an international crisis, through the administration and civil service of a global power, and through His chosen man, Joseph, who now finds himself unexpectedly at the centre of the world stage. Events, which in the biblical world-view are never as random as they appear, bring Jacob's family before the greatest man in Egypt after Pharaoh himself, setting the stage for a rather bizarre family reunion. God uses Joseph to bring his family to true repentance and then to save them from death by famine. God wants us to understand that He is concerned not only to save their lives but also to save their souls, and that repentance is essential if that is to happen. That is the real purpose behind this detailed account of Joseph's experiences in the book of Genesis.

As we read the Old Testament, we need to understand that at root God is addressing the human heart and the fundamental human need for people to have a right relationship with God. We see that illustrated here. Jacob's family need food in the midst of a famine, but they need something much more. They need to be changed by the power of God if they are ever to fulfil their destiny to be the people of God, the light of the world and the ancestors of the Messiah. The opening verses of the book of Hebrews provide us with the lens through which to interpret the Word of God. It says that in 'many and various ways' God spoke to our forefathers through the prophets.[1] Throughout the course of history God has been interacting with humanity, first through Adam, the representative man, then through Israel, the representative nation, and now through the church of Jesus Christ. Both Adam and Israel failed to be what they were called to be, but Christ came as the last Adam and as the true Israel to undo the failure of the past, to fulfil the Abrahamic covenant with God and to establish a new covenant by His blood. So as we read the story of Israel, we find God dealing with them as a race and as a geopolitical nation, but also as needy men and women needing to be transformed into His likeness.

The crisis

After Joseph's interpretation of the king's dream, everything came true just as he had foretold. There were seven years of bountiful harvests, as predicted,[2] before the years of famine.

The famine was severe in all the world.[3]

---

[1] Hebrews 1:1-2
[2] Genesis 41:47-8
[3] Genesis 41:57

As we hover in the wings of the Egyptian palace watching these events unfold, we wonder what is going on back in Canaan. Will they be affected by this great problem?

The last time we saw the family of Joseph back home in Canaan they were a far from happy lot. They were divided among themselves and Jacob was mourning uncontrollably for Joseph. Now, in chapter 42, the plot tension centres on the family's survival. They are not an attractive bunch. Simeon and Levi were guilty of having slaughtered the unsuspecting people of Shechem many years before. Reuben, the oldest son, had committed incest with his father's concubine, and Judah had a child by his daughter-in-law. Some might say that it was the family from hell! Yet the amazing thing is that in the last book of the Bible, when the Holy City comes down out of heaven from God, the names of these brothers mark the twelve gates of the heavenly city[4] – the names of the twelve tribes of Israel. What did it take for God to transform these scheming, sinful brothers into the revered founders of God's chosen nation?

Crises can either pull a family together or make it fall apart. Certainly the family of Jacob doesn't look very happy in this time of crisis. What was the problem? First, there was the famine.[5] Famine is always tragic and we see images of famine in Africa on our TV screens all too often. It was bad back then too. But there was hope in this famine. Jacob had heard that there 'was grain for sale in Egypt.'[6] What the family didn't know was that God had been at work over the past twenty years setting things up just so that they would be saved from death.

---

[4] Revelation 21:12
[5] Genesis 41:57
[6] Genesis 42:2

What is hard to explain is the inaction of the sons. Their father has to say to them, 'Why do you just keep looking at each other?'[7] Sometimes things that happen in life are so big, so overwhelming, so seemingly insoluble, that they leave us in a state of paralysis, not knowing what to do. We freeze up. But these men have not been noted in the past for their inability to take appropriate action, especially when their own well-being was at stake! So how is it that since there is a famine and there is grain available in Egypt, they are sitting around looking at each other?

Of course we know what these brothers knew. They had a guilty secret. The last time they had seen their long-lost brother, he was being carted down the road to Egypt by a group of Ishmaelite traders. The very mention of Egypt must have seared their consciences. You can imagine them looking guiltily at each other, Judah looking at Reuben, Simeon looking at Levi, while Issachar furtively glances at Gad. As Shakespeare said, 'Conscience does make cowards of us all.'[8] If there had been anywhere else in the world to go to find bread, they would have gone there like a shot, but Egypt? The very mention of that word stirs their consciences. So the old man has to dress them down and shake them from their lethargy. He trusts God, but he also calls for action. Jacob knows from experience that God's blessings don't come automatically to the lazy.

But there is another strike at their consciences. There is an element of mistrust in the way their father acts. Jacob doesn't send Benjamin with them for fear something might happen to him.[9] Was it that he wasn't sure about these

---

[7] Genesis 42:1
[8] Shakespeare, *Hamlet* Act III scene I
[9] Genesis 42:3-4

brothers? It probably wasn't the first time their father had shown such distrust in them and each time must have been like a slap in the face to these men. They knew well enough why their father was holding back. It was not only that he was protective of the only remaining child by his dear wife Rachel; it was that he also could not trust them. He had no idea what had happened to Joseph, but he had no doubt about the brothers' guilt. They could hide their crimes, but not their characters. Whatever reason Jacob had for mistrusting them, their minds would invariably go to their involvement in Joseph's disappearance.

Goaded by their father, the brothers eventually set off to Egypt, with their past sins casting a shadow over them. There is one important aspect of the way this journey to Egypt is described which is worth noticing. This is the first time a connection is made with Israel, the name God had given Jacob and which was to be the name of the chosen nation:

> *Thus the sons of Israel came to buy among the others who came, for the famine was in the land of Canaan.*[10]

The Severity of God

Now Joseph was the governor of the land, the one who sold grain to all its people. So when Joseph's brothers arrived, they bowed down to him with their faces to the ground. As soon as Joseph saw his brothers, he recognized them, but he pretended to be a stranger and spoke harshly to them. 'Where do you come from?' he asked.[11]

Words can wound, but sometimes as they wound they can also heal. We find them doing this very thing here.

---

[10] Genesis 42:5
[11] Genesis 42:6-7

Joseph, whom we have already seen representing God's word in Egypt, is now used by God to wound with a view to healing his brothers. We, who know the story well, know the outcome. Joseph has been sent ahead by God, though he doesn't know it, to save this family.

Robert Candlish wrote that, in his opinion, if Joseph had been left to himself, he would have revealed his identity in a moment, but he was restrained by God, who was using him for the salvation of his brothers.[12] Scripture tells us that Joseph remembers his dream,[13] and suddenly he realises that their arrival in Egypt is no coincidence, it is the hand of God. He remembers his role as God's servant. He then acts in full realisation of his calling, which God had already revealed to him in dreams. He had been called to lead his father's house, to save it from death and bring it back into the paths of righteousness. Joseph is not looking for revenge, nor does he punish anyone. He tests his brothers to see whether he can trust them, and to find out whether there has been any change in attitude. He is used by God to bring them to repentance and a real change of mind, heart and action.

It's been twenty years since the brothers last saw each other. Back then Joseph was a bearded seventeen-year-old Hebrew lad, probably sun-bronzed. The tan would have gone, as Egyptians of the elite class stayed out of the strong sun (pale was cool), and he would be clean-shaven too, which was a distinctively Egyptian look. What about hairstyle? I have an image of black hair, square cut with a long fringe, Cleopatra style – that would certainly be an excellent disguise! Now he looks like an Egyptian, walks

---

[12] Robert Candlish, *Studies in Genesis*, 652
[13] Genesis 42:9

and talks like an Egyptian and, more importantly, is one of the top officials in the land. His brothers were certainly not expecting to see him and nothing in his manner gave him away. Could it be that Joseph hoped to see his family, since he seems to have taken an active interest in the sale of grain to foreign visitors? Did he come down to the sales point every day and search the faces of the many visitors who poured into Egypt, looking for anyone who might seem familiar? On the other hand, he might have been there simply as a normal part of his job. We can't know for certain. If he was on the look-out for his family, why when they finally appear does Joseph not immediately make himself known? Is he being spiteful? Not according to the text. It says two things. First it says that he 'remembered the dream' he had of them.

Then he *remembered* his dreams about them and said to them, 'You are spies! You have come to see where our land is unprotected.'[14]

Perhaps over the years, Joseph had forgotten the afflictions in his father's house, but as he recognizes his brothers and they bow down to him, he now remembers the dreams.

Secondly it says he was 'testing' them.

"And this is how you will be tested: As surely as Pharaoh lives, you will not leave this place unless your youngest brother comes here."[15]

He wants to see whether they have changed.

Joseph challenges his brothers' integrity

Egypt had always been at its most vulnerable from its north-eastern border. In fact a huge canal ran down from the Mediterranean Sea to Lake Timsah as a defensive line.[16] There was also a network of fortresses that lined this eastern border. Egypt was as security-conscious then as most nations are today, so the charge of spying out the land was not a bad pretence for trapping the brothers.

Three times Joseph accuses them of being spies.[17] The charges come raining down like hammer blows, threateningly trying to break down their resistance. They have come to spy out the unprotected parts of the land, he says. They strenuously deny any such behaviour.

'No, my lord,' they answered. 'Your servants have come to buy food. We are all the sons of one man. Your servants are honest men, not spies.'[18]

Do you see the double irony of their reply? 'We are all sons of one man,' they say. Without realizing it, that was true, because the official standing before them was also their brother! They realise that their character is on the line, so they defend their integrity. In their response, the word they use to describe themselves is 'honest', which means literally 'just', so they are claiming to be just men. Of course it was precisely in this that they had failed miserably, and Joseph was only too aware of that! One thing they were not was either just or honest. They had been lying to their father for years now about the fate of this very brother who, unknown to them, is standing in front of them. In other

---

[15] Genesis 42:15

[16] Currid, *Genesis*, 282

[17] Genesis 42:9-14

[18] Genesis 42:10-11

words, here the Word of God, through Joseph, can be seen pressing on the pus-point of sin in their lives.

Joseph accuses them once again of being spies,[19] and without waiting for more lies he puts them in prison to meditate upon what he has said and to come to terms with their former sin. He is teaching them that God is against them just as they had been against their brother in the past. Sometimes God has to use severe methods before we face up to what we truly are. Although these brothers had been dishonest to their dad all these years, now, for the first time, standing in front of this official in Egypt, they begin to be honest with themselves and with him.

When we think of our Lord Jesus as the one God has exalted to rule over His church, and we remember that 'no creature is hidden from his sight, but all are naked and exposed to the eyes of him, to whom we must give an account,'[20] it ought to fill us with a due sense of humility and holy fear.

Joseph challenges his brothers' loyalty

Honesty is one thing, but loyalty takes relationships to a different level, and Joseph's brothers were not distinguished for having either love or loyalty to their family. Now it would be easy to moralise about the importance of loyalty generally here, but that would be to miss the point. This was no ordinary family. Remember that this was the family through whom God intended to bless the world in accordance with His promise to Abraham. It was also the family through whom the Messiah was to come in God's good time. The spiritual dimension of their attitudes and

---

[19] Genesis 42:14
[20] Hebrews 4:13

behaviour is therefore of real significance. Ultimately it is their relationship with God which is at stake.

Scripture does not tell us how the brothers felt as they cooled their heels in prison, but they probably expected to be there for a considerable time. No doubt to their amazement, they are suddenly released after three days. Joseph's tone has changed as he outlines the conditions on which they are being freed and explains his reason:

> On the third day, Joseph said to them, 'Do this and you will live, for I fear God.'[21]

He is teaching them about his own conscience. His conscience is governed by his fear of God, and he is putting the claim of God before them, telling them indirectly that they should also fear God. As one hymn puts it,

> Fear him ye saints
> And you will then
> Have nothing else to fear[22]

The Word of God confronts these men. This is in line with Joseph's career so far. Whether in Potiphar's house, confronted with the overtures of his wife; or in the prison when speaking to his fellow prisoners; or in front of Pharaoh insisting on giving God glory for his gifts, Joseph consistently bears witness to God. He is God's word in Egypt, being heard by everyone who comes into contact with him. So he puts his actions in the context of his godly fear. By reversing his decision because he fears God, Joseph

---

[21] Genesis 42:18
[22] Nicolas Brady (1696), 'Through all the changing scenes of life'

is modelling to them the kind of response God wants from them. They too can change their ways if they act in accordance with godly fear.

Joseph's condition for their release is that he will keep back one of their group until they return with their younger brother, challenging them to prove their earlier assertion that they were 'honest men'. [23]

'If you are honest men, let one of your brothers stay here in prison, while the rest of you go and take grain back for your starving households. But you must bring your youngest brother to me, so that your words may be verified and that you may not die.' This they proceeded to do. [24]

Joseph did no more than the apostle Paul did for the Corinthians when he wrote to them about the effect of his previous letter:

> *Even if I caused you sorrow by my letter, I do not regret it. Though I did regret it – I see that my letter hurt you, but only for a little while – yet now I am happy, not because you were made sorry, but because your sorrow led you to repentance. For you became sorrowful as God intended … Godly sorrow brings repentance that leads to salvation and leaves no regret, but worldly sorrow brings death.* [25]

The question here in Genesis is whether this will turn out to be a 'godly sorrow' that leads Jacob's sons to repentance. Will there be evidence of God's Word wounding them? As the story goes on, we see evidence that the Word is beginning to get through.

---

[23] Genesis 42:11
[24] Genesis 42:19-20
[25] 2 Corinthians 7:8-10

As the brothers try to get their heads around this surprising turn of events, they say to one another,

'Surely we are being punished because of our brother. We saw how distressed he was when he pleaded with us for his life, but we would not listen; that's why this distress has come upon us.'[26]

In effect they are saying, 'we are guilty and are being punished.'[27] Their guilt is real. They acknowledge that guilt and punishment belong together, so they are able to recognise a higher hand in their present misery. This is happening to them 'because of our brother,' they say. They see their developing circumstances as evidence of 'God's higher justice matching their punishment with their crime against Joseph'.[28]

This is an important admission, for it gives us an insight into the faith of these men. In spite of everything else we can say about them, they believed in God. They believed in His moral government of the universe. They believed that crime and punishment belong together. They recognised that they were reaping what they had sown. In the New Testament the apostle Paul gives us this warning:

Do not be deceived; God is not mocked, for whatever one sows, that will he also reap.[29]

William Perkins explains what this means like this:

There are two sorts of seeds which men sow in this life, good and evil. Two kinds of sowers; spiritual men and carnal men. Two

---

[26] Genesis 42:21
[27] Waltke, *Genesis*, 547
[28] ibid, 548
[29] Galatians 6:7

sorts of ground in which this seed is sown; the flesh and the spirit.
Two sorts of harvests which men are to reap according to the seed;
corruption, and life.[30]

Here they were, at a point in time far removed from their original actions, reaping the consequences of those actions. This is a salutary warning to us all. Some of us have sown seeds of *lust* and reaped a harvest of immoral behaviour. Others have sown the seeds of *vaulting ambition* and have reaped a harvest of broken relationships and bitter memories. Some of us have sown the seeds of *deception* and have lived to reap a harvest of mistrust.

Our present conduct determines our future condition. Ultimately we have to bear the responsibility for our own behaviour. Thus the old saying is true: 'Sow a thought, reap an act; sow an act, reap a habit; sow a habit, reap a character; sow a character, reap a destiny.'[31]

Joseph has been speaking to his brothers through an interpreter, so they have no idea that the top man in Egypt can speak Hebrew. The atmosphere is emotionally charged as they admit to one another how wrong they had been to ignore Joseph when they threw him into the pit. True repentance begins with a change in the way we think about things. These brothers are at long last beginning to think and reason in a spiritual manner. Somehow the passage of time has softened them. In fact you can see a contrast in the way they refer to Joseph in this chapter. Before, they had referred to him as 'that dreamer'.[32] Now they speak of him as their 'brother' and also, with a tinge of affection, as 'the

---

[30] William Perkins, A Commentary on Galatians, 496

[31] Philip Ryken, *Galatians*, 257

[32] Genesis 37:19

boy' or 'the child'.[33] Back in chapter 37, we read nothing of the begging cries of their brother. But we do here:

'We saw how distressed he was when he pleaded with us for his life, but we would not listen.'[34]

Now those cries were ringing in their ears. Joseph also now finds out that Reuben had not been supportive of the way they had treated him.[35] That must have been reassuring. Perhaps for the first time in twenty years, they were finding the courage to face up to what they had done; and they were sorry. Here is the beginning of their repentance, their turning back.

Before we are ready to feel the medicine of God's love being poured into our hearts, we too must face up to our sin. That is why the confession of sin is so crucial to Christian life and worship. It is the recognition that we can never be of any use to God or to our fellow humans until we have acknowledged what we really are. It will do us no good to pretend that our faults and failures in the past are due only to mistakes or our circumstances, upbringing or environment. The apostle John writes:

If we claim to be without sin, we deceive ourselves and the truth is not in us. If we confess our sins, he is faithful and just and will forgive us our sins and purify us from all unrighteousness.[36]

Contrary to today's popular wisdom, guilt is not always bad. It is good to feel bad about something we have done

---

[33] Genesis 42:13, 22
[34] Genesis 42:21
[35] Genesis 42:22
[36] 1 John 1:8-9

that is bad, for only then can we begin to move forward. Here the severity of the way these men are being handled awakens their consciences in a way which a brother's cries and a father's distress had never done. God is moving in their hard hearts. Conscience, under the prodding of God's Word, is a mighty tool to bring us to repentance. In the words of Andrew Fuller:

> It…is God's officer and vicegerent in man; set by him to be, as it were, thy angel, keeper, monitor, remembrancer, king, prophet, examiner, judge – yea, thy lower heaven. If thou slightest it, it will be an adversary, informer, accuser, witness, judge, jailer, tormentor, a worm, rack, dungeon, unto thee – yea, thy upper hell![37]

The kindness of God

So far the hand of God has been heavy upon these brothers. The rough edge of Joseph's tongue has pulled them up short and has begun to do its work of bringing them to their senses spiritually. But now there is a different feel to things. The Bible says that God always disciplines those He loves:

> My son, do not make light of the Lord's discipline, and do not lose heart when he rebukes you, because the Lord disciplines those he loves, and he punishes everyone he accepts as a son.[38]

We know that Joseph loves these brothers in spite of what they had done to him - this is why he weeps:

> He turned away from them and began to weep.[39]

---

[37] Quoted in Currid, *Genesis*, 285

[38] Hebrews 12:5-6

[39] Genesis 42:24

He has been looking for evidence of a change in these men, and he begins to see it. He senses a change in their spirit and he wants to treat them kindly while ensuring that they will return with the rest of his family. So Joseph chooses Simeon to be held prisoner as a guarantee of their good faith until such time as they return with Benjamin, and sends them on their way.

Joseph gave orders to fill their bags with grain, to put each man's silver back in his sack, and to give them provisions for their journey.[40]

In doing this, Joseph becomes the conduit of the kindness of God to these men, showing both compassion and wisdom in his dealings with them. When they discover the money in their bags on their way home, does it look like kindness to them? Do they not rather think it is a trick or trap? Astonishingly, for the first time in the whole story of Joseph, the brothers mention the name of God.

They turned to each other trembling and said, 'What is this that God has done to us?'[41]

The guilt which had been aroused by the words of Joseph, makes them see the hand of God in this act of kindness, and that makes them afraid.

Even God's kindness to us can make us afraid sometimes. When we are far from Him and living in conscious disobedience to Him, we find no pleasure even in little acts of kindness or evidences of His provision. Even the goodness of God tastes stale to the disobedient mouth; we wonder why He should be so kind. Joseph's brothers could see the hand of God in all this. Perhaps it was Joseph's treatment of them that made them reflect on God's goodness to them

---

[40] Genesis 42:25
[41] Genesis 42:28

and their own sin against Him. Their fear is a godly fear. It comes from God's grace and generosity towards us. As the hymnwriter and former slave trader John Newton wrote, 'Twas grace that taught my heart to fear.'[42]

God is both kind and severe. He wants to bring us to a change of mind and heart and life so that we can enjoy His salvation. Joseph acts as God's servant here. He shows kindness and severity so that this family can be changed and then saved from death and become a great nation in Egypt. The apostle Paul writing to the Romans, asks the unrighteous:

> *Do you presume on the riches of his kindness and forbearance and patience, not knowing that God's kindness is meant to lead you to repentance?*[43]

In the case of these men, Joseph's act of generosity was a hint of God's kindness and severity. They realised, as they had never realised before, that God knew everything there was to know about them. I remember hearing some people say of some divinity students at Edinburgh University, 'those men know all there is to know about God except that he is listening to them.' These brothers of Joseph suddenly became aware that their whole lives had been lived under God's eye. 'What is this that God has done to us?' They couldn't escape it!

Watch this space!
When they reach home, Jacob listens to his sons tell their side of the story. Then as they open their bags and he sees the silver, he begins to wonder. Had they stolen the grain?

---

[42] 'Amazing Grace'
[43] Romans 2:4

They did look guilty. Why would an unknown Egyptian want their younger brother brought back there? How could they go back if they hadn't paid for the grain the first time round? Jacob slumps into self-pity, 'Poor me,' he says in effect. 'Everything is against me!'

And Jacob their father said to them, 'You have bereaved me of my children: Joseph is no more, and Simeon is no more, and now you would take Benjamin. All this has come against me.'[44]

Everything is left up in the air. This is a good way to tell a story. Come back next week for the next exciting episode! Tune in next week and see what's going to happen next! Will Simeon languish in prison for long? Will the brothers ever develop character? Will Jacob continue to wallow in his self-pity? Will he ever be able to trust his children again? What is going to happen?

Then Reuben comes up with a great idea — 'kill my two sons if I don't bring him back.'[45] Up to now this man has been frankly self-serving. Now, however inept it may appear, he is putting his own family on the line. Is it a sign of hope that he is prepared to give up something for his brother; is family love and loyalty gong to emerge at last? Watch this space!

It is amazing that God could work with a not-very-nice family like this. We should be grateful if we live in families where we are loved and where our parents are prepared to sacrifice themselves for us. But above all we should be grateful that God was prepared to sacrifice Himself, in His son the Lord Jesus, for our salvation and eternal happiness. We have consistently seen Joseph as a picture of the Lord

44 Genesis 42:36
45 Genesis 42:37

Jesus, and we see something of the character of Jesus in his actions here also. Like Joseph, Jesus was rejected by His own people, who cried out in Pilate's court, 'We don't want this man to be our king.'[46] Similarly, just as Joseph was exalted to the highest place available in Egypt, so Jesus was exalted to the highest place in the universe:

> God exalted him at his right hand as Leader and Saviour to give repentance to Israel and the forgiveness of sins.[47]

Just as Joseph was exalted in order to be in a position to lead his brothers to repentance and safety, so Jesus was exalted to bring repentance to Israel and, indeed, to bring repentance to all of God's people. From His throne, Jesus puts his finger on our consciences. He speaks deeply into your life and mine. He identifies the sin we would rather forget, so that we might confess it to Him and find true and lasting forgiveness. Jesus has come to deal with our guilt before a holy God. Sometimes He has to use severe mercies to bring us back to Himself.

As this chapter ends, we are beginning to see the birth of those things which will make the reconciliation of these brothers possible. We see the birth of faith, true confession of sin, tender emotion and developing loyalty. In His kindness and severity, God is bringing them to repentance. As Joseph challenges their integrity and their loyalty, he brings them to a place of repentance. He does for them what Jesus does for us by the Word and Spirit. Jesus enables us to see the depths of sin in our hearts so that we might learn to appreciate the grace of God in the gospel.

---

[46] Luke 19:14.
[47] Acts 5:31

It's your kindness that leads us to repentance, O Lord.[48]

Jacob seems to have given up on his kids, but God hasn't given up on His purposes for them. And He doesn't give up on us either.

Can a mother's tender care Cease toward the child she bare? Yea – she may forgetful be, Yet will I remember thee.
Mine is an unchanging love; Higher than the heights above, Deeper than the depths beneath, Free and faithful, strong as death.[49]

One contemporary Christian song puts it like this:

Waiting for angry words to sear my soul,
Knowing I don't deserve another chance,
Suddenly the kindest words I've ever heard
Come flooding from God's heart.

It's your kindness that leads us To repentance,
O Lord, Knowing that You love us
No matter what we do
Makes us want to love You too.

No excuse, no one to blame, No way to hide,
The eyes of God have found my failures, Found my pain.
He understands my weaknesses And knows my shame
But His heart never leaves me.
If You are for us Who can be against us?
You gave us everything, even Your only Son.[50]

---

[48] L Phillips 'Your Kindness'
[49] William Cowper
[50] L Phillips 'Your Kindness'

8

No such thing as a free lunch

Have you ever sensed how quickly we slip into complaining when life doesn't go our way? Some of us will immediately blame God for life's inequities. Others of us are too spiritual to blame God when things go pear-shaped so we blame the church instead. The church wasn't there when you needed it; the people who go there are not all they could be; you don't feel as accepted as you should; no-one gives you the attention or the place you long to enjoy. Have you ever complained like that? Do you feel like that today? Things have become tough for you and you are looking around for someone to blame. The more you think about it, the more you sink into a mire of negativity.

One of the reasons we sink into negative thinking is that we cannot see the big picture of life. That isn't our fault, of course, since we are human and only God is God, but if we are believers we are expected simply to believe! One of the reasons for studying the life of Joseph is that his experience is faith-building for us. Although he is able, eventually, to articulate something of what God is doing through his trials, even he doesn't see the whole of the Bible's plot-line. It took the Lord Jesus coming into the world many centuries later to put Joseph's life into its bigger perspective. Jesus taught us to see all the Scriptures as bearing witness to Him. Luke 24:27 tells us about Jesus' conversation with some disciples after his resurrection:

> *And beginning with Moses and all the Prophets, he interpreted to them in all the Scriptures the things concerning himself.*

The Bible tells us about God and in particular bears witness to what God is doing through His Son, Jesus Christ. Out of the tragedy of humanity's rebellion against God, as told in Genesis, comes the promise of the 'seed of the woman' that would decisively destroy the evil one.[1] The rest of the Bible is the unpacking of that promise. First, through Adam's son Seth and then through one of his distant descendants, Noah's son Shem, the promise is narrowed down to the Semitic peoples.[2] Then Abraham is called and the promise is elaborated – through his seed the whole world will be blessed.[3] The bulk of Genesis then tells the story of his family and its development.

The story so far

Now anyone who reads the rest of the Bible will be surprised by the story as it unfolds in Genesis. Throughout the Bible God is pleased to identify Himself as 'the God of Abraham, Isaac and Jacob.' Jacob is also named Israel, and God is

---

[1] Genesis 3:15
[2] Genesis 4:26 and chapter 10
[3] Genesis 12:1-4

pleased to be known as the 'Mighty One of Israel.' When we read the Genesis story, we cannot help but ask, 'How can this be?' How can God bear to be identified with such a terrible family? As we have already seen, if ever there was a dysfunctional family, this is it. If ever there was an ungodly group of people, this is such a group. However you read it, they are a disaster. Here are blood brothers who have no love for one another and no regard for their father; who are capable of incest, immorality, deception and murder. Heartless and shameless, they are living in Canaan, the land of promise, but are beginning to lose their identity as God's people of promise altogether. Through intermarriage, not only is there a dilution of their line, but they are even adopting the gods of the Canaanites around them.

Why is this bad? Because, as the story will show, the salvation of the world depends on this family surviving and remaining recognisable as a people! One of the brothers, Judah, is destined to be the forerunner of Christ himself. So, how will these men ever be saved and transformed? How will this family be kept away from the Canaanite gods long enough to grow into a great nation? How will the seed from which God intends to ultimately produce the Messiah, be preserved from extinction? The story of Joseph is the answer. He is sent down to Egypt 'to save many people.' Psalm 105 says that God had 'sent a man ahead of them.'[4]

On the basis of the Bible's own explanation of what is going on in this story, it is clear that two things are happening – the *salvation* and *transformation* of these people. But how does God work this out for them? And

---

[4] Psalm 105:17

how can He work it out for us? It would be great if it were all straightforward, so that all He has to do is something dramatic. But He most often doesn't act like that at all. Usually our salvation and transformation is a work which for most of the time seems inexplicable to us. That is the simple reality of the Bible's teaching. For Joseph's family, this transformational process has begun, as we saw in the last chapter.

Danger – transformation at work
The story of Joseph in Genesis operates at several levels. It is helpful to pause for a moment and see the big picture. Famine conditions lead Joseph's brothers to go down to Egypt for food. We invariably think of such events as being outside the purpose of God. Someone asked me recently, 'If God can sometimes heal, why doesn't he sometimes stop tsunamis?' Well, the answer is that most tsunamis actually don't hit populated areas and most earthquakes cause no or few casualties because they take place in remote areas. Also, we have no idea how many of these tragedies God averts in order to spare us humans. But even if we did, I wonder whether we would be thankful. In the case of Jacob's family, the famine upset their comfortable life in Canaan and forced them to go to Egypt. This is a case of natural disaster being used in God's wider purposes.

On another level, God is working for, and then through, Joseph, even when he is enduring pain and suffering. Joseph is down in Egypt in God's purposes, to save his brothers, the children of Israel, and to preserve the family of the coming Messiah. He is raised up to the highest rank in the land so that he is in precisely the right place to help his people. Unknown to his brothers, the career of Joseph in Egypt is preparing the ground for their ultimate deliverance. When, eventually, the Saviour of the world is born, He is under threat of death at the hand of King Herod. Another Joseph, his legal guardian, takes Him down to Egypt to preserve His life.[5] An amazing parallel with the story of Joseph!

At yet another level, God is at work in Joseph's family. As well as the fact of Joseph being in the right place to save the rest of his family, an inward work of transformation has also begun in his brothers. To begin with, they have no regard for God or other people at all. In the first couple of chapters of their story, God is not mentioned and they are presented as a pretty callous lot. But then things begin to change.

Unknown to them, they meet Joseph – now the most important figure next to Pharaoh in all Egypt – when they are buying food. The harsh treatment they experience at Joseph's hands unsettles them. They had never been treated harshly anywhere by anyone. Whenever anyone had done them wrong they had simply hit back, as they had with the people of Shechem![6] In Egypt, they are accused of being spies, then thrown into prison. At that point a dramatic change begins to occur. For the first time we hear these men confessing their sin:

> 'in truth we are guilty concerning our brother, in that we saw the distress of his soul, when he begged us and we did not listen. That is why this distress has come upon us.'[7]

But it takes an act of kindness by Joseph to help them take the next step towards transformation. He sends them home with their grain and puts the money back into their sacks.

---

[5] Matthew 2:13-15
[6] Genesis 34
[7] Genesis 42:21

This really shakes them, and they ask, 'What is this that God has done to us?'[8] Suddenly God is in their thoughts, and they recognise the kindness of God in this and, strangely, that unnerves them.

Joseph is raised up to the highest rank in the land, and in that position he is used to further the spiritual education of his brothers. God had used the humiliation of Judah at the hands of his daughter-in-law to make him see something of his own sinfulness, and now He uses this famine to strip all of the brothers of their self-confidence. He uses the harsh treatment of Joseph and their imprisonment to make them see what they had done that had been so wrong. He uses the generosity of Joseph in giving back the money they had paid for the food to teach them something of the generosity of God. The curriculum in God's school of correction is tough, and it's about to get worse before it can get better.

Does this help us to see how God works? He is often at work on different levels and through a variety of circumstances and people to accomplish a work in us. Those circumstances affect others besides us, and God is at work in and through them too. It is a testimony to our impatience that we frequently fail to recognise this, and we wonder why God doesn't immediately give us the blessing we seek. Why do we have to wait? Why do we have to go through such difficulties sometimes? These are the questions we so often ask, and the story of Joseph and his family helps to provide some answers.

---

[8] Genesis 42:28

Famine in the land

Food seems to be the focus of chapter 43. There is still no food in Canaan. Famine has gripped the land and things are becoming serious. However, there is a meal in Egypt; in fact the meal is nothing short of a feast. There is a deeper purpose to the story as it unfolds, however. As Moses tells the story, he spends time on some details which at first reading may seem unimportant, but which are included to emphasise the process of reconciliation that is going on. Circumstances are drawing this dysfunctional family closer together and setting the stage for the next scene in the drama of God's unfolding purposes.

The prospect of starvation highlights the seriousness of the family's condition. There is no sign of the famine abating, and the first lot of grain from Egypt is rapidly disappearing. Jacob looks a bit callous, allowing things to get so bad before suggesting that they go to Egypt again for help.

> *And when they had eaten the grain that they had brought from Egypt, their father said to them, 'Go again, buy us a little food.'*[9]

There are some events that grip us humans which strip us of all our pretensions to self-sufficiency and self-satisfaction. Famine is one of them. It brings us face to face with our own mortality and makes us aware of a greater power than our own in the universe. Perhaps that is why we invariably rage against God when things like this happen, even if we don't believe in Him.

Jacob is still technically the head of the family, but a subtle change is taking place. Judah is increasingly acting as the head. Eventually his tribe will become pre-eminent in

---

[9] Genesis 43:2

Israel. Reuben is sidelined, probably because of his sexual liaison with his father's concubine. Judah now assumes the place of leadership among his brothers. The severe mercies of the famine and Joseph's test coaxes the best out of him.[10]

Judah forcefully reminds his father of the conditions laid down by Joseph:

> *'The man solemnly warned us, saying, "You shall not see my face unless your brother is with you."'*[11]

The concept of seeing the 'face' was the language of the court, used of an audience with a ruler or high official. Joseph is referred to as 'the man', which suggests anonymity. The brothers don't know who he is, but the next part of the story will lead to their discovery of his identity. For now, what strikes Judah is the fact that their whole survival as a family depends on their relationship with this unknown Egyptian, and he knows only too well that this important figure wasn't kidding when he had insisted that they bring their brother Benjamin down with them if they ever wanted to do business with him again. When Jacob questions their wisdom in divulging that they had a younger brother, the brothers reply with deep agitation and regret in their voices.

> *They replied, 'The man questioned us carefully about ourselves and our kindred, saying, "Is your father still alive? Do you have another brother?" What we told him was in answer to these questions. Could we in any way know that he would say, "Bring your brother down"?'*[12]

---

[10] Waltke, *Genesis*, 552

[11] Genesis 43:3

[12] Genesis 43:7 Some have noted that these questions are not to be found in their first conversation with Joseph. However a look at ch.44:19 indicates that

How were they to know? You can sense their growing desperation, because by this time they do not want to lose their youngest brother.

Can people ever change? We often ask that question. Sometimes change comes ever so slowly. Let this next part of the drama be a reassurance to you that God can change even the hardest hearts and transform even the cruellest people. Don't give up on yourself or others too soon. Listen to Judah's plea and pledge:

> *Judah said to Israel his father, 'Send the boy with me, and we will arise and go, that we may live and not die, both we and you and also our little ones. I will be a pledge of his safety. From my hand you shall require him. If I do not bring him back to you and set him before you, then let me bear the blame forever.'[13]*

What a change in Judah! Judah speaks wisely and boldly to his father. He makes a pledge and invokes a curse on himself. He is risking his family fortune and even his life to save the rest of his family. Whereas Reuben had put his sons' lives on the line,[14] Judah puts his own life on the line. The expression 'I will bear the blame' is, in the original Hebrew, a word for sin, literally, 'I will have sinned.' If he violates the agreement, he will take whatever punishment Jacob sees fit. In as respectful but direct a way as he can, he gets his father to face the facts. They have no alternative.

Joseph had indeed asked these questions. In other words ch.42 does not report everything that was said but is selective.

[13] Genesis 43:8-9

[14] Genesis 42:37

A tough call for Jacob

It is at this point we begin to see a change in Jacob. He reluctantly gives in and allows Benjamin to go with them to Egypt, though there is a weary and despairing sadness in his voice. He does what he can to try to ensure a positive response from the great man of Egypt.

> *'If it must be so, then do this: take some of the choice fruits of the land in your bags, and carry a present down to the man, a little balm and a little honey, gum, myrrh, pistachio nuts, and almonds. Take double the money with you. Carry back with you the money that was returned in the mouth of your sacks. Perhaps it was an oversight. Take also your brother, and arise, go again to the man.'[15]*

It was customary for travellers to present gifts to a high official in a foreign land. These gifts were called 'choice products'. In this instance they included three products that formed part of the merchandise carried by the Ishmaelite caravan that had taken Joseph to Egypt over twenty years before. Ironically, it is almost a repeat of that scenario. On this occasion the brothers take the part of the merchants and Benjamin takes the role of Joseph as they bring him down to Egypt. It is ironic too that Joseph should now be given those same products as a gift by his brothers. Two of these, 'spice' and 'myrrh', are mentioned only in these two places in the Old Testament. They determine to give back the money they had found in their sacks. That was the ethical thing to do. These brothers are acting honestly and honourably at last.

The thing to notice here is the way Jacob talks about God. He shows faith, of course, by committing them to the mercy of 'God Almighty':

---

[15] Genesis 43:11-13

*'May God Almighty grant you mercy before the man, and may
he send back your other brother and Benjamin. And as for me, if
I am bereaved of my children, I am bereaved.'*[16]

He believes that God is ruler over all, that He orders all
things and that our lives are entirely in His hands. Is he
perhaps resigning himself to losing Benjamin too? Perhaps a
sense of fatalism gripped him, 'what will be will be'. Perhaps
we shouldn't be too hard on Jacob, though. The fact is that
our confidence in God frequently co-exists with our own
fearfulness and even hopelessness at times. God gives us the
grace 'to *doubt* and yet *believe* that he is really there.'[17] In the
end, Jacob surrenders himself to the will of God. Israel is
being Israel, a true prince with God once again.

Jacob has one more role to fulfil in this. He points the
brothers to what they and he and we most need, the mercy
of God. 'May God Almighty grant you mercy,' he says.
Mercy is the narrative key to this chapter. It is about the
mercy of God. We see it at work through Joseph, when
we read about Joseph's 'compassion' (literally 'mercy') for
his brothers later in the chapter.[18] Their father's prayer is
answered in the response of Joseph to their plight.

In his banqueting house?
The entire trip to Egypt is mentioned in one verse.

*So the men took this present, and they took double the money with
them, and Benjamin. They arose and went down to Egypt and
stood before Joseph.*[19]

---

[16] Genesis 43:14
[17] Joni Earecksen Tada, *A Step Further*, 123
[18] Genesis 43:30
[19] Genesis 43:15

It's as if the tension is being cranked up in the story. From now on events are going to move very fast. The next great move in the drama is the disclosure of the identity of the highest official in all Egypt.

As the brothers return to Egypt, they are unsure what will happen. They expect the worst. Remember, they had discovered the money they had used to pay for the goods lying hidden in their sacks. They had no idea how it had got there, and were worried the Egyptians would think they had stolen it. So they had good reason to believe that the authorities in Egypt would be keeping an eye out for these people who had in effect got grain for nothing on their first visit. Imagine their terror when they find themselves being treated like royalty, being washed and cleaned up and brought to the head man's home.

The men were afraid because they were brought to Joseph's house.[20]

What was going through their minds? Did they feel their hands wet with fear as they were ushered into his presence? We know from the text what was on their minds:

'It is because of the money, which was replaced in our sacks the first time that we are brought in, so that he may assault us and fall upon us to make us servants and seize our donkeys.'[21]

No wonder they suspected these tactics, since they had used somewhat similar ones in Shechem!

Their fear and Joseph's apparently friendly demeanour must have been unnerving. Three verbs sum up Joseph's commands, 'bring ... slaughter ... prepare'.[22] Did the use

---

[20] Genesis 43:18
[21] Genesis 43:18
[22] Genesis 43:16

of the word 'slaughter' make them more uneasy? And what an experience for these shepherds from the wild places, to be wined and dined by a high official in Pharaoh's court! They must have been getting increasingly nervous; they knew that there was no such thing as a free lunch. All the time they must have been thinking about the money in their sacks. We can imagine them saying to one another, 'When will it dawn upon the official? When will he realise he was defrauded? Does he already know and does he have plans to 'fall upon' us with force?' All the time they must have been thinking that the Egyptians were bound to regard them as thieves. So before they go in to the banquet, they speak to the chief steward and tell him the story of how they discovered the money in their sacks. No-one has accused them of anything, but they come up with their excuse before they are even charged.

> 'Oh, my lord, we came down the first time to buy food. And when we came to the lodging place we opened our sacks, and there was each man's money in the mouth of his sack, our money in full weight. So we have brought it again with us, and we have brought other money down with us to buy food. We do not know who put our money in our sacks.'[23]

The nervousness is evident in their voices as they try to explain what had happened.

Nothing could have prepared them for the steward's response. He is gracious and friendly:

> 'Peace to you, do not be afraid. Your God and the God of your father has put treasure in your sacks for you. I received your money.'[24]

---

[23] Genesis 43:20-22
[24] Genesis 43:23

Not only are they not condemned men, but there is no charge to answer. The chief steward's response is couched in theological language. 'Peace to you,' means literally 'shalom', a word meaning 'harmony', 'well-being' and 'happiness'. It is repeated three times.[25] 'God has blessed you,' he says. 'I on the other hand have been compensated. Legally you have nothing to worry about.' This word 'shalom' is a very important word in the Bible. It is the great purpose of God to bring us to experience this peace. They probably couldn't believe their own ears. Here was a pagan steward assuring them that their guilt had been covered, their debt had been paid, and that they had nothing to answer for. They were now guests of the great man himself and could sit down at the table with him with a clear conscience and full assurance. As a Christian believer, I too find myself in the presence of greatness, the glorious God. I am in great debt to God, yet I discover that my debts are paid and I am cleared to enter His presence.

As if to make sure they knew they were in the clear, the steward then reunited them with Simeon, who had been left as surety for their good faith on their previous visit.

Once assured of their status, the brothers probably had peace of mind to go through the social preliminaries before they entered the presence of the great man himself. Joseph, like any aristocrat of the period, received them and their gifts with great formality.

He inquired about their welfare and said, 'Is your father well, the old man of whom you spoke? Is he still alive?' They said, 'Your servant our father is well; he is still alive.' And they bowed their

---

[25] See also Genesis 43:27, where it is translated 'how is'

heads and prostrated themselves. And he lifted up his eyes and saw
his brother Benjamin, his mother's son, and said, "Is this your
youngest brother, of whom you spoke to me? God be gracious to
you, my son!" [26]

We can only imagine what it must have been like for
Joseph to maintain the masquerade for so long and now to
see his youngest brother, who had been but a lad when he
had last seen him. Moses gives us an insight into the deep
emotions that Joseph felt:

Joseph hurried out, for his compassion grew warm for his brother,
and he sought a place to weep. And he entered his chamber and
wept there. [27]

It is deeply moving to see how much Joseph is affected
by seeing his younger brother after such a long time. He
has to go off on his own till he recovers. He must have
been tempted to reveal who he was at that point, but
shows remarkable self-control. There were still lessons
his brothers needed to learn and Joseph needed proof of a
change of heart.

After composing himself, Joseph calls for dinner to be
served:

They served him by himself, and them by themselves, and the
Egyptians who ate with him by themselves, because the Egyptians
could not eat with the Hebrews, for that is an abomination to the
Egyptians. [28]

---

[26] Genesis 43:27-29
[27] Genesis 43:30
[28] Genesis 43:32

This is evidence of Moses' familiarity with Egyptian practices. Joseph eats separately because of his rank and adopted race. The Egyptians eat separately because they had an ethnic, religious and national sense of their own importance. In fact, because the Hebrews were shepherds, that was another reason for keeping them at a distance, because shepherds were an abomination to Egyptians. To their amazement, the brothers are seated according to their order of birth. No wonder if they are bewildered by what is going on!

Their host is generous to a fault. He lulls them into a state of relaxation, but he also loads Benjamin with attention. By showing favouritism, he is replaying the old problem. Will his favour to Benjamin arouse envy and jealously in his brothers? In all this there is an insight into the providence of God. Just as Joseph has privileged knowledge and directs events to achieve a good purpose, so does God. Joseph is a picture of the sovereign God in this story. Just as he is generous to them and at the same time unsettles them, so God often does the same to us

I hope you see the parallel between the brothers and ourselves. We too are on the receiving end of God's great generosity. In theological language we call it *common grace*. This is grace that comes to everyone, irrespective of whether they are God's people or not. Jesus referred to it in these terms:

For he makes his sun rise on the evil and on the good, and sends rain on the just and on the unjust.[29]

---

[29] Matthew 5:45

The fact is that we humans take for granted the generosity of God and yet all we can do is complain when something is withheld from us or something unwelcome is thrown our way. The rest of the time, we are ungrateful and don't give Him a thought. We see this around us in the wealth and affluence of our part of London. All these things people have, including us, come from God. But do we thank Him? The fact is that God does not owe us anything. Or if He does, it is to judge us for our sin against Him. What is amazing is that He doesn't destroy this planet altogether. Today some of us here who are not Christians will go home and eat well, tonight we will sleep well and tomorrow we will not wake up in hell. At least not yet! Isn't that amazing? Why is God so good to those who never thank Him or even think about Him until something happens which they think they can blame Him for? The answer is this: it is to bring us to repentance. He is good to all He has made. It is the tragedies of life which remind us that for most of humanity, most of the time, there is abundant provision, and yet still we disregard Him.

God's presence and identity are often hidden from us, just as Joseph's was from his brothers. We see only part of the picture. We wonder why things happen as they do and we think they are random events, or we think they are arbitrary circumstances. It would have been easy to wonder, 'What is going on here?' Are there things in your life like that? These brothers did not see the emotions which Joseph felt. Rather they saw his 'hard' side. They saw the 'tough' Egyptian and only we are given to see the tears shed in silence out of sight. Sometimes the tenderness of God is hidden from us too.

In my experience we are too ready to give up on God or, if that is a step too far, on His people, the church. Of course no church is perfect. If it were, it would soon be rendered imperfect if you or I joined it!

Do you know these words by John Newton?

I asked the Lord that I might grow
In faith, and love, and every grace;
Might more of His salvation know,
And seek, more earnestly, His face.

'Twas He who taught me thus to pray,
And He, I trust, has answered prayer!
But it has been in such a way,
As almost drove me to despair.

I hoped that in some favored hour,
At once He'd answer my request;
And by His love's constraining pow'r,
Subdue my sins, and give me rest.

Instead of this, He made me feel
The hidden evils of my heart;
And let the angry pow'rs of hell
Assault my soul in every part.

Yea more, with His own hand He seemed
Intent to aggravate my woe;
Crossed all the fair designs I schemed,
Blasted my gourds, and laid me low.

Lord, why is this, I trembling cried,
Wilt thou pursue thy worm to death?
'Tis in this way', the Lord replied,
'I answer prayer for grace and faith.'

These inward trials I employ,
From self, and pride, to set thee free;
And break thy schemes of earthly joy,
That thou may'st find thy all in Me.[30]

As this chapter ends, Benjamin is being plied with food and gifts, and any of the old envy has gone as they all enjoy the experience together:

And they drank and were merry with him.[31]

Another kind of grace has begun to work in their hearts.

---

[30] John Newton, 1779
[31] Genesis 43:34

9

Putting it back together again

Have you noticed a subtle shift in thinking among Christian people over the last few years? Today Christian living is often described in terms of 'gifts' – that is, what I do, how I function in the body of Christ, what I might contribute to the body. Others define it in terms of 'temperament' – what are my personality traits? Indeed candidates for the ministry are likely to have to undergo all kinds of tests to ascertain whether they have the right temperament to be a minister. Amazingly, there is no reference to personality or temperament in the Bible. Its great emphasis is on character. We see this in the story of Joseph's brothers. They had great character flaws, but as the next scene of this drama unfolds, God brings about a sea change in the lives of these men. So far they have acted very badly, but now they start to act nobly. This change in them is evidence that God is at work.

Repentance at work

There comes a point in everyone's life when choices and actions of the past have to be faced up to. They can be ignored, of course, suppressed, explained away or excused. Or they can be confessed and put behind us. In Jacob's family there was long-term underlying rivalry between the children of four different mothers. Just two of the twelve boys were born of Rachel, the wife Jacob truly loved. The others resented them for that. So much so, in fact, that in the past they had got rid of Joseph, one of Rachel's sons, or so they thought.

Now the question is this, have these brothers changed? They have been subjected to a series of tests. They have had to cope with the privations of severe famine. In order to buy the food they need to survive, they have suffered the humiliation of bowing down before the most powerful man in Egypt after the Pharaoh, who is actually their brother Joseph. They have been tested by this brother they fail to recognise. Behind all these testing situations, God is setting about the task of making these men fit for His service.

A couple of poignant moments indicate how much their thinking has begun to change. They have confessed honestly to one another their guilt and wrongdoing with regard to Joseph.[1] And having brought Benjamin back with them, they have accepted his being spoilt by the great man of Egypt without the slightest hint of envy or hostility.[2] Unknown to them, it is Joseph who is testing the sincerity of their hearts. This is a reminder that we cannot always see what God is up to. We see some things that make us think He is hard or doesn't care. We may at times even feel

---

[1] Genesis 42

that He is against us. So often, however, we fail to see the evils He saves us from; the benefits of common grace He gives us from day to day; and His heart of love that weeps for us and which wants only our good. Some trials are tests of obedience, of love, or willingness to sacrifice for Him. As I look back over my life, I see many times I have failed such tests, and it grieves me. I find myself saying with the hymnwriter, 'I hate the sins that made thee mourn.'[3]

These men had failed tests of character in the past, but over time grace was slowly doing its work in them. This family has been under the rod of God. That rod of discipline has been applied through circumstances and through the actions of an unknown Egyptian official, who seems to have taken an extraordinary interest in them. Joseph has been setting them up to see how they will respond when he gives preferential treatment to Rachel's second son, his own blood brother, Benjamin. Now, in chapter 44, Joseph tightens the noose in yet another test to see just how much his brothers have changed.

After the brothers have bought grain, Joseph orders that their money be put back in their sacks for the second time, and in young Benjamin's sack the officials were also to put Joseph's own silver cup, no doubt a very valuable item.[4] The brothers haven't got very far on their journey home when Joseph's steward catches up with them and accuses them of stealing the silver cup.[5] So sure are they of one another that they deny it outright and even invoke the death penalty on anyone found with the cup.[6] Earlier in their lives it is

---

[2] Genesis 43

[3] William Cowper, 'O for a closer walk with God'

[4] Genesis 44:1-2

[5] Genesis 44:3-5

[6] Genesis 44:7-9

unlikely they would have felt so sure of each other. When the planted silver cup is discovered in Benjamin's sack, they are beside themselves with grief. They act as one man and turn back to Egypt, refusing to abandon Benjamin. This is another hint in the narrative that these are changed men. Wenham writes:

> *when Joseph disappeared it was only Jacob who tore his clothes (37:34); now all the brothers do, the first sign of fraternal solidarity.*[7]

There is a definite change in them.

Joseph is very subtle at this point. His steward calls the cup a 'cup of divination', that is a cup used by people of high status in Egyptian life as a technique for finding out the truth.[8] We know that Egyptians used such cups for various forms of magic, so perhaps the brothers would not be surprised to learn of such a practice, but of course Joseph is using this word 'divination' in an entirely different way from the Egyptians. He wants to establish the truth about their attitudes. Through this cup and their being brought back, Joseph is going to discover for sure where they are spiritually.

The journey back to Joseph's house could not have been easy; their minds must have been in turmoil! The first thing the brothers do is to throw themselves at Joseph's feet. They know that their lives are on the line. They admit their corporate guilt and try to establish their innocence. Notice what Judah says as their spokesman:

---

[7] Wenham, Genesis,
[8] Genesis 44:5

'What shall we say to my lord? What shall we speak? Or how shall we clear ourselves? God has found out the guilt of your servants, both we and he also in whose hand the cup has been found.'[9]

They insist that they are not guilty in this instance, but they confess their guilt, because they remember their abuse of Joseph.

In the Bible such a total reorientation of life is called repentance. The process began in chapter 42, when the brothers first went to Egypt and were thrown into prison as potential spies. They immediately thought about the brother they threw into a pit and they owned up among themselves to their sin. Now it is evident that this admission was more than simple remorse. It was a genuine confession of sin. Confession of sin means to give God glory by acknowledging sin and God's right to punish it. It was the beginning of true repentance, which involves a change of mind, of heart and of direction. Such confession of sin is essential to an enjoyment of God's forgiveness. In the New Testament this point is made by John:

If we confess our sins, he is faithful and just and will forgive us our sins and cleanse us from all unrighteousness.[10]

Just to test the sincerity of their repentance, Joseph gives his brothers one last chance to escape at Benjamin's expense:

'Only the man who was found to have the cup will become my slave. The rest of you can go back to your father in peace.'[11]

---

[9] Genesis 44:16
[10] 1 John 1:8-9
[11] Genesis 44:17

This is the point at which the tension is palpable. What will they do? Will they abandon Benjamin? They have come back with him to face the music; that was a good sign. But suppose they have a way out, will they take it? Once again a test is put before them.

It might be thought that this is a very harsh thing for Joseph to do to them. They certainly have a hard choice to make, of that there is no doubt. But the upshot of it is going to be a stronger family bond and the personal transformation of this group of people.

Grace at work

Judah's speech in response to Joseph's insistence that only Benjamin should be held to account for stealing the cup is the longest in Genesis, occupying sixteen verses, and it is a masterly piece of work. In fact it is probably one of the most moving speeches in human history. It is succinct, full of pathos; it is also humble and heartfelt. Judah emerges as the hero of the family at this point.

There are two particularly important aspects to his speech, an act of intercession and an offer of substitution.

First, there is an act of intercession. Once before, he had stepped in and advised his brothers to 'sell' Joseph,[12] but on that occasion there had been no humanitarian motive to his actions. We know his brother Reuben did not want to have Joseph killed, because the text says so,[13] but the text doesn't tell us that Judah was marked by any spirit of altruism at all. He had an eye for a good deal; get rid of Joseph once for all and make some money into the bargain. Now he steps up and refuses to 'sell' Benjamin. His speech reveals the extent

---

[12] Genesis 37:27
[13] Genesis 37:22

to which this man has changed. It also shows him to have the kingly qualities needed to rule over his brothers.

There is a new sensitivity to their father. In fact the word 'father' is repeated several times. Before this they had little thought about how their father would feel if they got rid of Joseph. They had lived for over twenty years in the shadow of Jacob's grief, and now they are concerned to spare him further pain. Judah even tries to imply that Joseph will be complicit in causing Jacob's death from grief.

> 'As soon as he [Jacob] sees that the boy is not with us, he will die, and your servants will bring down the grey hairs of your servant our father with sorrow to Sheol.'[14]

It seems that the brothers have come to terms with the special love their father had for his wife Rachel. Judah's mother Leah had been 'forced' on Jacob, and his liaisons with the maidservants of his two wives had been motivated by convenience, in order to have more children. In this speech Judah speaks of the favouritism Jacob showed to Rachel's two boys without rancour or blame. But in particular there is a heartfelt plea for Benjamin's freedom. They have found a genuine love for this their youngest brother. Judah is actually interceding for his brother before Joseph, and he is making it clear that they will not desert him under any circumstances:

> 'For your servant became a pledge of safety for the boy to my father, saying, "If I do not bring him back to you, then I shall bear the blame before my father all my life."'[15]

---

[14] Genesis 44:31
[15] Genesis 44:32

Those who know their Bibles will recognise the work of someone else reflected here. Judah's greatest descendant is none other than Jesus Himself. One of His great works is to intercede for His people before God.

He ever lives to make intercession for us.[16]

We find Jesus interceding for us in John 17, where He prays for all those who will believe in Him through the message of the apostles and asks that they will be protected from the evil one and brought safely home to glory so that they may see and share in the glory of God.

> *Before the throne of God above*
> *I have a strong and perfect plea.*
> *A great high Priest whose Name is Love*
> *Who ever lives and pleads for me.*
> *My name is graven on His hands,*
> *My name is written on His heart.*
> *I know that while in Heaven He stands*
> *No tongue can bid me thence depart.*[17]

Second, there is an offer of substitution. Having spoken for them all, Judah now speaks for himself:

> *'Now therefore, please let your servant remain instead of the boy*
> *as a servant to my lord, and let the boy go back with his brothers.*
> *For how can I go back to my father if the boy is not with me? I fear*
> *to see the evil that would find my father.'*[18]

Judah is putting himself in harm's way for Benjamin's sake. Judah is willing to be a slave himself rather than let his brother be enslaved. There is great grace in his words and

---

[16] Hebrews 7:25
[17] Charitie L. Bancroft, 1863
[18] Genesis 44:33-4

in his offer. This man has changed beyond recognition. Dr
Donald Gray Barnhouse puts it like this:

> *Here is the eloquence of true love. Love so burningly manifest, so
> willing to take full responsibility before God, love which thought
> only of Jacob and Benjamin, melted the heart of Joseph. Such love
> moved Moses to ask God to blot his name out of the book of life
> (Exodus 32:32); such love prompted Paul to wish himself accursed
> for his brethren if only they could be saved. Judah was transformed
> by divine love.*[19]

Judah is the first person in the Bible 'who willingly offers his
own life for another. His self-sacrificing love for his brother
for the sake of his father prefigures the atonement of Christ,
who by his voluntary sufferings heals the breach between God
and human beings.'[20] His descendant Jesus would actually
offer Himself as a sacrifice and substitute for His people. This
Messiah would become known as 'the Lion of the Tribe of
Judah'.[21] In the Messiah's kingdom, the King himself sacrifices
himself for the least and lowest in his Realm.

What Joseph does is to create a situation in which his
brothers come face to face with some of the same choices
they had confronted so many years before, when they had
decided to get rid of the irritating lad in the multicoloured
coat. This 're-enactment' enables the brothers to prove
their conversion, both to Joseph and themselves. Jesus
asking Simon Peter if he loved Him, once for every time he
had denied Him, comes to mind as an example of a similar
confirmation of a radical transformation.[22]

---

[19] Barnhouse, *Genesis*,
[20] Waltke, *Genesis*, 567
[21] Revelation 5:5
[22] John 21:15-17

Jacob will crown Judah with kingship[23] because he demonstrates that he is fit to rule. He shows the ideal of kingship here, one who serves rather than needs people to serve him.

Providence at work

It is the realisation of how far these men have changed that opens the floodgates of Joseph's pent-up emotions. What follows at the beginning of chapter 45 is an outpouring of emotion and affection. For the first time he can be real with them. When his brothers begin to take in what he is saying to them, they are at first fearful. After all, the brother they had sold as a slave is now one of the most important and powerful men in all Egypt, the superpower of their day. Joseph invites them to draw near.[24] He doesn't deny their responsibility for their actions; they are indeed guilty. It never helps anyone to deny or cover up guilt at such moments. Yet he has compassion on them and comforts them. Even after all he has been through, Joseph forgives his brothers. One of the first results of sin confessed is the privilege of drawing near to God, knowing that our sins have been forgiven.

As he acts to calm their fears, Joseph voices the theology that undergirds this whole story: God has been sovereignly at work to accomplish His purposes.

> 'And now do not be distressed or angry at yourselves because you sold me here, for God sent me before you to preserve life.'[25]

---

[23] Genesis 49:10
[24] Genesis 45:4
[25] Genesis 45:5

This is the key to the whole Joseph story. It is in fact a story about God. It is Joseph's understanding of this that makes him able to forgive. After all, people might think he had every reason to take revenge for all these men had done to him. Yet he responds with compassion and mercy; he embraces them and loves them. How can he do that? Because he believes in the sovereignty of God!

Throughout this book, Joseph has proclaimed God's Word in Egypt. In chapter 39:9 Joseph said to Potiphar's wife:

> *'How could I do such a wicked thing and sin against God?'*

When the king's cupbearer and baker asked him to interpret their dreams, Joseph made it clear that this is something only God can do

> *'Do not interpretations belong to God?'*[26]

When he was brought before the king and hailed as one who could interpret dreams, he set the record straight:

> *'I cannot do it ... but God will give Pharaoh the answer he desires'* and *'God has revealed to Pharaoh what he is about to do'*[27]

He even named his sons with reference to his God. Manasseh means 'God has made me forget all my troubles,' and he chose Ephraim because 'God has made me fruitful.'[28] Joseph related everything to God. Now he does so again as he comforts his brothers:

---

[26] Genesis 40:8
[27] Genesis 41:16, 25
[28] Genesis 41:51, 52

'But God sent me ahead of you to preserve for you a remnant on earth and to save your lives by a great deliverance. So then, it was not you who sent me here, but God. He made me father to Pharaoh, lord of his entire household and ruler of all Egypt.'[29]

Right at the beginning of the story, Joseph was sent by his father to see to the welfare of his brothers. Neither he nor his father could have dreamt how that task was going to be accomplished. In fact, God was going to use Joseph to see to the welfare of both his own family and the whole world. Four times Joseph describes himself as God's agent.[30] Notice Joseph's emphasis on God: 'God sent me before you to preserve life' (v5); 'God sent me to preserve for you a remnant' (v7); 'so it was not you who sent me here, but God' (v8); and 'God has made me lord of all Egypt' (v9). Providence has been at work, and providence is God's good government of the world in the interests of His people and for His glory.

The outworking of God's providence
The story of Joseph raises questions of God's timetable. He doesn't always work as quickly as we might like. It takes thirteen years of slavery and prison before Joseph is elevated. Even once he is established as an interpreter of dreams, it is two years before Pharaoh has a dream which stirs the cupbearer's memory and gets Joseph out of prison. God doesn't always work to our calendar.

The story of Joseph raises questions of God's purposes. These are explained in terms of a 'remnant'. God was at work 'to preserve life' (v5) and 'to preserve for you a remnant on

---

[29] Genesis 45:7–8
[30] Genesis 45:5, 7–8; 42:25; 43:23

earth, and to keep alive for you many survivors' (v7). Right from the beginning of Genesis and the announcement of a seed,[31] there has been this unfolding purpose to save God's people with a great deliverance. God's purpose is to protect and preserve His people so that they will not be destroyed but saved. This deliverance through Joseph was only to be one in a number of such rescue operations. All of them pointed forward to the final and decisive rescue achieved by Christ on the cross.

The story of Joseph raises questions of God's ways. Think of the incident of the money in the sack. When the brothers open their sacks and find the money, they immediately think that God is punishing them. When they get back to Egypt, Joseph's steward explains to them that the silver is in fact God's gift. What they see as God's action against them is in fact a blessing in disguise.

The bottom line is that God is so in charge of this world that 'his sovereignty and blessing can be found in what seem to be the most heinous crimes and the most disastrous circumstances.'[32] This does not mean that God approves of evil. Nor does He enjoy our suffering. But it does mean he can bring good out of evil. He doesn't suppress our choices, but none of our choices, however bad, can interfere with His plan. This can be seen in the way Joseph juxtaposes 'you sold me ... God sent me' (v5) and 'not you ... but God' (v8). He understood that every episode of his life and theirs had been under God's direct rule.

God did not approve of what the brothers had done. 'You meant it for evil,' says Joseph,[33] not downplaying for

---

[31] Genesis 3:15
[32] John Walton, *Genesis, The NIV Application Commentary*, 696
[33] Genesis 50:20

one moment their motives. Nor did God make them do it. They were totally responsible for their own actions. He did not need them to be bad like this in order to achieve His purpose. But out of their bad behaviour and even worse choices, God brought something good for them and the world.

Now Joseph tells his brothers that God used their wickedness for His own purposes in order to comfort them. In fact, all the episodes of Joseph's story contribute to demonstrating how God's purposes are ultimately fulfilled through and in spite of human deeds, whether or not those deeds are morally right.[34] This is supremely true of the cross. There wicked men did what *they* wanted to do with the Son of God, yet amazingly, in doing their will, they were working out *His* will and purpose. It is knowing God to be sovereign, knowing that He is in charge of history and destiny, that makes all the difference.

> Careless seems the Great Avenger; history's pages but record
> One death-grapple in the darkness 'twixt old systems and the word;
> Truth forever on the scaffold, wrong forever on the throne, –
> Yet that scaffold sways the future, and, behind the dim unknown,
> Standeth God within the shadow, keeping watch above his own.[35]

There is no greater comfort for us as believers than knowing that God is governing our lives, and that God has a bigger plan than we can see. Some of us may be despairing over

---

[34] Wenham, *Genesis* 16–50, 432

[35] James Russell Lowell, *The Present Crisis*, in Masterpieces of Religious Verse, ed. J. D. Morrison (New York: Harper and Brothers, 1948).

some bad choices we have made. We may be torn by grief or remorse. We may think we have screwed up big time and pulled others down with us into our mess. But we mustn't think for one moment that God has stopped working or that He cannot work out His own will even in and through our bad choices. God's hand directs through all the confusion of human guilt and human weakness and human wickedness.

This is what Moses most wants us to learn from Joseph's story.

For our part, waking up to our sins should drive us back to Him in repentance and gratitude for His great grace, 'grace that is greater than all our sins.'[36]

The apostle Paul sums up the message of this chapter wonderfully:

> *where sin increased, grace abounded all the more, so that, as sin reigned in death, grace also might reign through righteousness leading to eternal life through Jesus Christ our Lord.*[37]

---

[36] Julia H Johnson, 'Marvellous Grace of our Loving Lord'
[37] Romans 5:20

10
A Perfect Day

There are days in life which cannot and must not be forgotten. These are occasions that are so touching, so memorable, that they remain vividly in the mind and imagination. So crucial are they, that they need to be talked about late into the evening for years to come and savoured again and again. Like a rich wine, such days need to be tasted and rolled around the palate. We sometimes call such days 'perfect days'. Do you have such days in your life?

Some time ago, I revisited some friends in Canada, where I had been pastor many years ago. I hadn't seen some of these folk for twenty-five years. We know that time wreaks havoc on us all, but this visit heightened my sense of my own mortality as I saw what the passage of time had done to folk! Yet when we got together, we talked and laughed and time flew by, and it was as if the years had rolled back and we were all young again and that no time had passed. For me, those were 'special days and hours'.

Genesis chapter 45 introduces us to such a day, the day

in Egypt when Joseph introduced himself to his brothers. It was the last thing one would have supposed at the beginning of the story – the family reunited and peace breaking out between the brothers!

Radical renewal

There are no obviously supernatural miracles recorded in the story of Joseph, yet true repentance is a miracle to beat all miracles. The change in Joseph's brothers is truly remarkable, a sign of God's grace at work in them. In the last chapter we looked at Judah's speech to Joseph in which he pleaded for mercy. His willingness to sacrifice himself on behalf of Benjamin marks a complete turnaround in this man and is a mark of true nobility of character. It is a lesson to us never to write anyone off. Radical change is evident in all the brothers, however. Not only are they being saved from death by starvation in the famine, but they are being saved from themselves; they are radically renewed.

Now this is consistent with the Bible's overall witness. God is in the business of saving and transforming people. Usually this transformation is not an overnight event, although that is the kind of thing we all tend to look for in life. We try the cream that helps us lose our wrinkles and look in the mirror next morning expecting to see a difference. Of course, it never works like that, if it works at all! In the same way, in the spiritual realm, the renewal of men and women is not the work of a moment or an hour; it's not usually something that happens suddenly in a crisis of 'complete surrender'. It is more often a work that takes place over the long term, as the Spirit of God does His work within us, gradually weeding out the roots of sin in our hearts and loosening our grip on this world and its values. In reality, that is what is going on behind the scenes in this story. The spirit of Jesus pervades the whole scene. It is the spirit of Jesus in the brothers that makes them willing to put themselves in harm's way in order to stand by their youngest brother Benjamin. It is the spirit of Jesus that makes Judah offer himself as a substitute and slave in his brother's place. And it is the spirit of Jesus in Joseph that gives him the grace to forgive his brothers unconditionally for all they have done to him.

Emotion released

We have to try to read ourselves back into that era. Egyptians were far worse than we Brits at expressing their true feelings. They practised that inscrutability that hides all emotion behind a façade of 'coolness'. Joseph himself had obviously had to take on the character traits of his adopted nation, but he hadn't completely lost his ability to express his emotions. Earlier, when he had overheard his brothers admit for the first time their wrongdoing in getting rid of him, he had slipped off on his own to weep silently, so moved was he.[1] But in public he had shown that control which would be expected of someone in such a high-profile job. He had been inscrutable, reserved and self-controlled.

All that is about to go by the board on this memorable day when the brothers appear before him a second time wanting to buy grain. Joseph dismisses his staff and the interpreters through whom he has been communicating with his brothers and introduces himself to them. There is something truly moving about the account of Joseph

---

[1] Genesis 43:30

giving vent to the pent-up emotions of more than twenty years of rejection, loneliness, slavery, wrongful accusation, unjust imprisonment, and even eventual success, yet there is something almost amusing about the biblical account:

And he wept aloud, so that the Egyptians heard it, and the household of Pharaoh heard it.[2]

He must have made such a fuss, but who could blame him? What love he must still have had in his heart for his father and even for his brothers; how deep the hurt of rejection must have gone; how great his joy must have been at the reality of being reunited and reconciled to his brothers. A complex confusion of emotions must have been released in him, but perhaps above all he would have known heartfelt satisfaction at seeing the evidence of their true repentance, a real change of heart and mind and direction in these brothers of his. It may come as a surprise to us that the dominant emotion he felt for them was love. That is not said directly in the text, but it can be inferred from his attempts to comfort them and draw them close to him.

Some of us have baggage from our past, but it has left us bitter and resentful. What we need is for God to work his miracle in our hearts, enabling us to love the guilty as God has loved us. The Bible has a word for this – 'grace'. Grace is about showing love to unworthy offenders. In God's case, He shows love and mercy to us in spite of the fact that we have offended Him by sinning against him. In our case, grace is our responding with love and mercy to those who have hurt or offended us, when anger and

---

[2] Genesis 45:2

judgment would be the expected reaction. How do we do that? There was grace made available to Joseph, and there is such grace available to Christians. The grace of the Lord Jesus is stimulated within us as we look to Calvary, where He bore our sins in His body on the tree. There we see our Lord taking the place of His guilty people, and in spite of our ingratitude and rebellion, securing our relationship with God. Meditate on the wounds of the Saviour and know it was for you He died, and see whether the more you meditate on Him, the more you treasure and value and love Him, till you are so grateful for His love for you that you must be gracious to those who have injured you.

God meant it for good

Here is a man who has spent a large part of his life reflecting on God's ways with him. When his story began, we saw Joseph sharing with his family what he believed was God's plan for them all. That plan is now in the process of being fulfilled. Now he explains the bigger picture of God's work in their lives and in history. He speaks not to prove a theoretical point, but to give them comfort. Like the apostle Paul in his letter to the Corinthians,[3] Joseph comforts them with the comfort he had received from God:

> *'God sent me before you to preserve life ... God sent me before you to preserve for you a remnant ... So it was not you who sent me here but God ... God has made me lord of all Egypt.'*[4]

Here is a statement of biblical realism. There are two aspects to every event in our lives. On the one hand, there

---

[3] 2 Corinthians 1:4
[4] Genesis 45:5b, 7a, 8a, 9b

is human mishandling or what we choose to call the blind working of nature, and on the other there is the perfect will of God. The way of true freedom from the tyranny of our circumstances is to see the will of God behind the events of our lives. This is what put things in perspective for our Lord Jesus. In the Garden of Gethsemane, as He prayed before His arrest, He agonised, as any of us would do, over the dreadful events that were about to unfold. But out of that agony He accepted the betrayal, the trial and the cross as 'the cup my Father has given me'.[5]

God has a good purpose for our lives. It is faith to believe that. Joseph had believed it for years and it had sustained him during the times when there was no obvious indication that such a view was true. Believing in the providence of God makes us able to rise above our circumstances rather than be victims of them. In the book of Proverbs we read:

> The heart of man plans his way, but the LORD establishes his steps.[6]

Sometimes people are doubtful about the value of theology or doctrine, especially the doctrine of God as sovereign. God's sovereignty refers to His right to rule His world as He pleases. Some of us trip up at this. Occasionally it is the events of life that make us doubt it. Why should bad things happen to good people? Don't you think Joseph could have asked that question? Yet it was this view of God that kept Him going through all those years. It was a high view of God's purposes and character. Our problem too often is that we think of God as altogether like ourselves. We

---

[5] John 18:11
[6] Proverbs 16:9

project on to Him our own little perspectives and our finite wisdom and our short-term strategies. We really think he should act as if we humans were the centre of the world and the purpose of the universe. This is our basic sin of course. We make ourselves in a thousand ways the centre of the world. Humanity is turned in on itself. In fact, it's the most wonderful relief to be knocked off our little throne and yield to the sovereignty of One who has the right to rule.

I want you to comfort yourself with the doctrine of God's sovereignty today. I want you to find peace in the fact that He can overturn your bad decisions; that He can cover your faults; that He can blot out your transgressions; and that He can retrieve good out of evil. Do you believe this?

Now it would be true to say that Joseph's brothers had been shown great mercy by Joseph even before they knew who he was. He had provided for them and given them all they needed. Both his severity and kindness had led them to repentance; that is, to a change of mind and heart. Now the process of reconciliation moves a stage further. Joseph sets the tone by urging them to come close to him:

> *Joseph said to his brothers, 'I am Joseph! Is my father still living?' But his brothers were not able to answer him, because they were terrified at his presence.*[7]

It is important to deal with this theme this way round. It was Joseph's theology applied to his own circumstances that made it possible for him to forgive. God's truth released 'the will for constructive effort and the emotions

---

[7] Genesis 45:3

for healing affection'.[8] It is when we are ignorant of God's ways with us that we are most likely to nurture hatred and nurse grievances. It is accepting the sovereignty of God that releases us to forgive.

The medicine of forgiveness

> *Then Joseph said to his brothers, 'Come close to me.' When they had done so, he said, 'I am your brother Joseph, the one you sold into Egypt!'*

Do you see the grace and tenderness of God acting towards these men through Joseph? Those words, 'come near to me,' speak of great tenderness, a warm welcome and acceptance. Conviction of sin is a terrible wound, but God does not want to destroy us by it, rather he wants to draw us close to Himself and heal the rift between Him and us. He wounds us to heal us.

We can well understand the profusion of emotions experienced by Joseph's brothers at this point. Chrysostom, one of the early preachers of the church, wrote:

> *I am surprised at the way they could stand there and gape without their soul parting company with their body, without their going out of their mind or hiding themselves in the ground.*[9]

So it was an uncomfortable moment for them. Coming to terms with our sin often is. It is when we realise that we have sinned against God, who has done us so much good, that we also face up to the depths of sin in our hearts.

Joseph, however, immediately applies the medicine of forgiveness to his brothers:

---

[8] Kidner, *Genesis*, 206

'And now, do not be distressed and do not be angry with yourselves for selling me here, because it was to save lives that God sent me ahead of you.'[10].... Then he threw his arms around his brother Benjamin and wept, and Benjamin embraced him, weeping. And he kissed all his brothers and wept over them. Afterward his brothers talked with him.[11]

We can understand Joseph getting all emotional about meeting Benjamin, his full blood brother who had no part in his rejection, but he goes beyond that. He embraces and kisses all his brothers.

In the language of his theology, that is, his understanding of God's way of working, Joseph is quite clear that God has overruled their sin and their evil intentions. He does not hold them to ransom. He does not insist on them paying for their sins. He is gracious and welcoming. Archbishop William Temple once wrote:

To return evil for good is devilish. To return good for good is human. To return good for evil is divine.[12]

In this we see a reflection of the spirit of Jesus. You will remember that on the cross he prayed for his executioners:

'Father, forgive them, for they know not what they do.'[13]

Realistic forgiveness
True forgiveness can co-exist with total realism and honesty. Joseph said:

---

[9] Mark Sheridan, ed., *Genesis 12-50*, Vol. 2, Ancient Christian Commentary on Scripture (Downers Grove, IL: InterVarsity Press, 2002), p290

[10] Genesis 45:5

[11] Genesis 45:14

[12] www.ccel.org/s/schaff/history/2_ch08.htm -

[13] Luke 23:34

'I am your brother Joseph, the one you sold into Egypt!' (Gen. 43:4).

You will notice that in true forgiveness there is no denial of wrongdoing. Some misunderstand forgiveness in this way. True forgiveness is being able to look the offender in the eye, acknowledge their offence and forgive them anyway. Here Joseph's intention is to tell them what only they and he knew, so as to verify his identity and to complete the joy of their restoration. It had to be mentioned, the questions and doubts in their minds about his intentions towards them had to be dissolved

Later, when he sends them back to Canaan, Joseph gives them some advice. 'Don't argue on the way,' he says.[14] He was being realistic, because on their way home these boys would know they had to come clean about their past crime to their father. In such a scenario, they might be tempted to argue with one another about who was or was not to blame for what they had done.

Peter once came to Jesus and asked Him:

'Lord, how often shall my brother sin against me and I forgive him? Up to seven times?'

Peter was getting the idea that forgiveness was a good thing, but at this point it was all a matter of calculation. He was wondering how many times it would be enough to forgive someone. Jesus responded by saying:

'I do not say to you, up to seven times, but up to seventy times seven.'[15]

---

[14] Genesis 45:24
[15] Matthew 18:21-22

Jesus is telling Peter that forgiveness is a matter of the heart.

At a personal level, the question is whether there is someone in our life whom we need to forgive or from whom we need to receive forgiveness. As for the church of Jesus Christ, it should surely be a forgiving community. After all, we regularly pray the Lord's Prayer and are reminded of its central plea, 'forgive us our debts as we forgive our debtors'. We are all God's debtors. Sin is debt we cannot pay, but which God is graciously pleased to forgive. We cannot do anything to repay the debt we owe. We just don't have enough moral strength to do it. That is why so many people are struggling with forgiveness. They think it is something they can drum up from deep inside themselves. Actually, forgiveness is impossible apart from the grace of God. In fact it is those who have been forgiven themselves who are best placed to know how to forgive others. How do I demonstrate the fact that I have been forgiven by God? I forgive other people! Dr Martyn Lloyd-Jones put it like this:

> *It means that the proof that you and I are forgiven is that we forgive others. If we think that our sins are forgiven by God and we refuse to forgive somebody else, we are making a mistake; we have never been forgiven. The man who knows he has been forgiven, only in and through the shed blood of Christ, is a man who must forgive others. He cannot help himself. If we really know Christ as our Saviour our hearts are broken and cannot be hard, and we cannot refuse forgiveness. If you are refusing forgiveness to anybody I suggest that you have never been forgiven ... I say to the glory of God and in utter humility, that whenever I see myself before God and realise something of what my blessed Lord has done for me, I am ready to forgive anybody anything. I cannot withhold it; I do not even want to withhold it.*[16]

---

[16] Lloyd-Jones, *Studies in the Sermon on the Mount*, Vol.2, 75, 76

Of course it costs. This act of forgiveness cost Joseph dearly over twenty years or more. It cost him rejection by his own people; the humiliation of going from being a well-loved son to a slave; the misrepresentation and false accusation of an enemy; and being cast into prison and left there to be forgotten for a while until God raised him up out of prison and exalted him over all the land.

Ultimately, forgiveness costs the life blood of the Son of God. When the New Testament says that 'we are justified by his grace as a gift through the redemption that came by Christ Jesus,'[17] it means that He was paying the debt we owed to God on our behalf. This is what makes the gospel 'good news'. It is about what Jesus has done freely and fully for us and about our need to simply take the forgiveness He offers us.

Perfect ending to a perfect day

As Joseph embraced all his brothers, all the guilt had gone. Joy had won the day. As they relaxed with each other, they no doubt talked and talked long into the evening. It was the end of a perfect day. He took the time to reassure them, in much the same way that our Lord Jesus, after His resurrection, took time with the disciples to reassure them of who He was and of His continued love for them, in spite of their desertion and in particular of Peter's denial. We have a picture of a new family, a new community of the forgiven and the reconciled. It is a picture of what the church should be, a place where fallen and sinful people find themselves accepted and included once again.

With the brothers reconciled, there is now an invitation from the king to all the children of Israel to come and

---

[17] Romans 3:24

enjoy the best of Egypt.[18] This event marks a turning point in the story. This stay in Egypt, facilitated by the Pharaoh, will allow the family to multiply and keep its identity. It will also lead to eventual bondage for the people and a deliverance that will forever teach this people and the world what it means to be redeemed as well as called. It marks the outworking of God's promise made long before in Genesis chapter 15, which accurately foretold these events:

> Then the LORD said to him, 'Know for certain that your descendants will be strangers in a country not their own, and they will be enslaved and mistreated four hundred years. But I will punish the nation they serve as slaves, and afterward they will come out with great possessions. You, however, will go to your fathers in peace and be buried at a good old age. In the fourth generation your descendants will come back here, for the sin of the Amorites has not yet reached its full measure.'[19]

Gordon Wenham writes like this:

> The God of Genesis is a God of mercy (43:14) and grace (44:29), who answered Jacob's forlorn prayer 'May God almighty grant you mercy from the man, so that he sends back your other brother and Benjamin' (43:14) beyond his wildest dreams. But in so doing, God is not just proving his control of events but keeping his promise to the patriarchs that they should have a multitude of descendants, or as Joseph puts it, 'a great number of survivors.'[20]

The land of Goshen, as it was called in Joseph's day, is called the land of Rameses in Moses' time. It lay east of the Nile delta and was very fertile. Twice it is described as the 'best'

---

[18] Genesis 45:16-28
[19] Genesis 15:13-16
[20] Wenham, *Genesis 16–50*, 433

or literally the 'good' of the land. This echoes the 'good' which God gives to Adam and Eve in Genesis chapters 1 and 2. Goshen is an echo of Eden. It is also a foretaste of the 'land of milk and honey' to which the people of Israel would one day come, the land of Canaan. And, in the bigger picture of the Bible, it is a foreshadowing of the new heavens and new earth that is the destiny of all of God's people.

The royal invitation given to a people near the end of hope, and to ten brothers burdened by guilt, can hardly fail to remind the Christian of God's gracious invitation to us.

Pharaoh said to Joseph, 'Tell your brothers, "Do this: Load your animals and return to the land of Canaan, and bring your father and your families back to me. I will give you the best of the land of Egypt and you can enjoy the fat of the land."'[21]

They are given the means of transport, all they will need for the journey. Joseph even gives them festive garments to wear:

To each of them he gave new clothing.[22]

The word used here suggests festive or celebratory clothes. Remember the coat of many colours? Was Joseph deliberately giving clothes in order to compensate in some measure for what they had failed to receive from their father so many years before? Now every brother is provided with new clothes as a sign of reconciliation.

The book of Genesis, after describing the creation of humanity, tells of its fall into sin. One of its first results was

---

[21] Genesis 45:17
[22] Genesis 45:22

the murder of one brother by another – Cain killed Abel. The book ends with a bunch of envious and rather nasty brothers being transformed and reconciled to one another. In other words, God's rescue package for the world has been put in place. This is what he is about. Here is the spirit of Christ at work in the hearts of individuals and families to restore and heal the damage sin causes in human lives. This is the only hope for humanity. We cannot legislate for this. It must come by an inner transformation made possible because God's appointed and anointed One has been elevated not to a position of power in an earthly kingdom, as Joseph was, but to the supreme place of power in the universe, where He rules our lives both for our good and His own glory. From that position He orders our lives and circumstances so that they challenge our assumptions, convict our consciences, change our minds and bring us to the place of reconciliation to Himself and to one another.

So the book of Genesis has a unified and well-designed structure. At the beginning there is a family torn by murder; at the end a family reunited by grace. At the beginning are people excluded from the Garden of Eden; at the end a people given a land that is a faint echo of Eden. At the beginning humanity is confronted with real guilt; at the end humanity learns of God's purpose to forgive. It is the New Testament which explains how such a transformation is possible. It points us to Christ, who is the great reconciler. It points to the creation of a new society where sinners are welcomed in and restored by the healing power of mercy and grace.

Martin Luther spends a lot of time on this incident in one of his sermons and notes that churches should be places like Joseph's home, where those who are guilty, lost and terrified find healing:

The churches are nothing else than lodging places of this kind in which the people who feel sin, death, and the terrors and vexations of an afflicted and wounded conscience are healed.[23]

We know the churches should be like this, but are they? Are they places where someone who has failed can feel welcome and be given the space to recover and grow? Are we, as individuals, people who treat others in that way?

---

[23] Quoted in Boice, *Genesis*, Vol.3, 188

11

Down to Egypt

A s we have reflected on the life of Joseph and his place in God's purposes at this time in the history of redemption, we have noticed various parallels with the life of our Lord Jesus. The fact that Joseph was used to feed Egypt and the world during the seven-year famine, offers another such point of comparison. The story makes it clear that God did this primarily to preserve the lives of His chosen people, the house of Israel. Just as the Egyptians had little concept of how much they owed to the God of Joseph, so the world today has no idea how much it benefits from the ministry of our Saviour and the presence of His people. His influence brings all kinds of benefits to the world of which it is not aware. There are the gifts of God's common grace, such as making the sun shine and the rain fall on both the godly and the ungodly, the righteous and the unrighteous. There is the preservative effect of Christians in society, holding back to some degree the tendency to corruption, restraining evil and encouraging good. Above all there is the work of the church in holding out the truth and pointing men and women to the Saviour. In every case, however, the world fails to see the grace that is shown to it. It takes the gifts but ignores the giver. Unbelievers are daily on the receiving end of countless blessings which God allows them to enjoy while they are in this world, although this is the only world they will enjoy. On the other hand, what God is doing in the world is being done primarily for the sake of His elect.

In addition to the prolonged famine, there was another threat to the family of Jacob, a spiritual one. The house of Israel was in danger of being absorbed into Canaanite culture and ways. The intermarriage that was going on among the sons of Israel and the women of Canaan is an indicator of this process. It was vital for God's chosen people to be separated from the Canaanites in order to maintain their identity and develop into a distinct people. So God used Joseph's elevation and the provision of food in the midst of famine to preserve His people both physically and spiritually at this time. Today of course He preserves His people not by physically separating them out of the world, but by first marking them out for Himself and then protecting them by his Holy Spirit from contamination by the world.

A gracious invitation

When Pharaoh hears of the arrival of Joseph's family, he is delighted and immediately invites the whole family of Israel to join Joseph in Egypt. He urges Joseph to shower his family with every inducement to come, and he backs up his invitation by sending carts to transport the brothers' wives, children and father:

And Pharaoh said to Joseph, 'Say to your brothers, "Do this: load your beasts and go back to the land of Canaan, and take your father and your households, and come to me, and I will give you the best of the land of Egypt, and you shall eat the fat of the land." And you, Joseph, are commanded to say, "Do this: take wagons from the land of Egypt for your little ones and for your wives, and bring your father, and come. Have no concern for your goods, for the best of all the land of Egypt is yours."'[1]

The brothers are under orders to act quickly. They are told to 'go' and 'enter'; they are not to delay, but are to get to Canaan and back as soon as possible The famine was so severe that delay might be life-threatening. Since things are so serious, they are not to worry about what they must leave behind. In any case, what they will get in Egypt will more than compensate for what they have to leave behind.

Joseph does what Pharaoh says and then goes beyond that, giving them more. He lavishes money on them and provides each of them with a change of clothes.[2] There is a touch of irony in this, for the trouble between him and his brothers had started with his father giving him a fancy outfit to wear. That fancy robe had caused only hostility. Now Joseph himself gives each of his brothers new outfits, but this time they symbolise reconciliation.

The change also symbolises their new situation: delivered from guilt, hostility, and famine, with the prospect of abundant provisions in the best of Egypt.[3]

All this provision and protection which Pharaoh offers is quite unusual. For Egyptians, shepherds and Asiatics were regarded as the lowest of the low, utterly to be despised. Why

---

[1] Genesis 45:17-20

[2] Genesis 45:22-3

[3] Waltke, *Genesis*, 572

should Pharaoh show such kindness to this family? It is due entirely to the character and worth of Joseph. It is his standing and his accomplishments that make the king show favour to these people. Is there a lesson here? I think there is. There is nothing in us that deserves or merits the mercy, far less the generosity of God towards us. His hostility is not based on prejudice, of course, but on our sin and rebellion against Him. It is because of the righteousness and work of another, namely our great representative Jesus who, like Joseph, was humbled before being exalted, that we are treated with great favour by God. This word 'favour' means the same as the word 'grace'. This story is overflowing with amazing grace.

The brothers' announcement

Considering the preoccupation with material things which has marked these men up to now, the way Joseph's brothers break the good news to their father on their return home is striking. Instead of giving a long list of all the goodies they have been given and a blow-by-blow account of how powerful and rich Joseph is and how their prospects are likely to improve if they move to Egypt, they focus on the personal and family aspect of it all.

> *So they went up out of Egypt and came to their father Jacob in the land of Canaan. They told him, 'Joseph is still alive! In fact, he is ruler of all Egypt.'*[4]

They are concerned to talk about their brother, not their riches. They are rejoicing in the fact that their brother 'is ruler of all Egypt'. Rather than being envious, they are proud of him.

---

[4] Genesis 45:25-26

This is an astonishing change in attitude, and appears to be a saving change. They have experienced the mercy of God through the generosity of their brother and his free forgiveness of them. They have learned something about God's sovereign grace. At the beginning of this story, it had rankled when their father had favoured Joseph over them, but no longer. When Joseph showed favouritism to Benjamin, they showed no resentment, in fact they were willing to put themselves in harm's way for him.[5] They have learned a vital lesson about God's electing love. God's grace is God's choice. He shows favour to whom He will. Whenever he shows mercy to us, it is not because we deserve it.

Wagon train

Jacob is stunned; 'his heart became numb, for he did not believe them.'[6] Literally, 'his heart grew cold,' he doesn't 'trust'[7] them. No wonder Jacob is resistant to their news and doesn't believe them! In part this is because he has learned to distrust his sons over so many years. After all, these are the ones who had come to him on that never-to-be-forgotten day, with Joseph's torn and bloodstained coat. No wonder he is reluctant to believe them or to see the evidence of a saving change in their lives. But perhaps he is beginning to wonder about them. There is something in their demeanour, something in their enthusiasm to speak Joseph's name, which certainly wasn't there all those years ago, which is making him think. There is joy in their voices and an excitement in their manner that carries conviction,

---

[5] Genesis 43:34; 44:33
[6] Genesis 45:26
[7] Currid, *Genesis*, 331

and anyway, who would make up a story like this if it weren't true?

> *But when they told him all the words of Joseph, which he had said to them, and when he saw the wagons that Joseph had sent to carry him, the spirit of their father Jacob revived. And Israel said, 'It is enough; Joseph my son is still alive. I will go and see him before I die.'*[8]

Do you see what made the difference? It says 'when he saw the wagons'. They must have been some wagons, because they changed his mind! They convinced him that it must have been Joseph they had met and that the brothers must be telling the truth. I don't know if they were Mercedes wagons or Bentley wagons, but they certainly got to him! It could very well be that he'd never seen a wagon in his life and that anyway these were top-of-the-range models. James Boice says it would be like landing a jumbo jet in a field somewhere in the jungle where people had never seen a car, far less a plane.[9] Actually, the more likely explanation is that Jacob reasoned with himself that they could have afforded to splash out on a few more donkeys, or that they could have stolen some donkeys, but to get such wagons as these you would have had to have been given them by someone important. These went way beyond their normal means. The wagons have an evidential value that build up Jacob's faith.

In the New Testament, it is the evidence of the *resurrection* of Jesus that builds faith. Jacob's response to the wagons reminds us of the response of the disciples when the women come with their news from the empty

---

[8] Genesis 45:27, 28
[9] James Montgomery Boice, *Genesis Volume 3*, Grand Rapids: Zondervan 1987, 203

tomb, saying that Christ is alive. Like the disciples, Jacob is at first stunned and sceptical of such improbable news. Then he is won over by the 'infallible proofs' (as Luke calls them[10]), just as the disciples were. There are several factors that lead people to believe that what we are saying about the Christian faith is true, but the resurrection is the most important evidence we have.

Back to Egypt

The narrator almost ignores the family's response to Pharaoh's gifts, because this family, which once was driven by the pursuit of material things and money, is now gripped by a higher calling and a deeper love. There is a restoration of family love and unity. There is a change in Jacob as well as in his sons. He is finally convinced that Joseph is alive, and prepares to move his whole family to Egypt. This is the man who had been prepared to sacrifice his relationship with his father and brother over material things in his younger days,[11] but this time he is not leaving home for the money, he is going to see his son.

> So Israel took his journey with all that he had and came to Beersheba, and offered sacrifices to the God of his father Isaac.[12]

Beersheba was as far as you could get in Canaan before leaving it, so it is here Jacob stops and worships, in the very place where his father Isaac had worshipped many years before.[13] You might think it was easy for Jacob to leave famine-blighted Canaan, but you would be wrong. He did not just

---

[10] Acts 1:3
[11] Genesis 25:29-34
[12] Genesis 46:1
[13] Genesis 26:23-5

assume, 'wherever I am, I can be happy because God is with me'. He clung on to Canaan because God had promised that land to him and his seed forever. Jacob was rightly concerned to be in the will of God as he considered going down to Egypt. His grandfather Abraham had gone down to Egypt and it had been bad news.[14] He had done it without consulting God and he had brought God's name into disrepute. So at Beersheba he offers sacrifices and worships. By doing this, Jacob identifies himself with the God of his fathers. He worships the same God. One reason he does this is because he knows himself to be a sinner in need of pardon. Every time the patriarchs offered sacrifices, they were acknowledging their offences before God and their hope of forgiveness through the better sacrifice that would one day come – which we know to be the Lamb of God who takes away the sin of the world.[15]

At Beersheba, God speaks to Jacob.

And God spoke to Israel in a vision at night and said, 'Jacob! Jacob!' 'Here I am,' he replied.[16]

James Boice talks about the few occasions in the Bible when God communicated with people in this way. When God interrupted Abraham as he was on the point of sacrificing his son, he said, 'Abraham, Abraham.'[17] When God called Samuel as a boy to be a prophet, he woke him at night by calling, 'Samuel, Samuel.'[18] Centuries later, when God stopped Paul in his pre-Christian days on the road to Damascus, he used his Hebrew name, 'Saul, Saul.'[19]

---

[14] Genesis 12
[15] Begg, *The Hand of God*, 174
[16] Genesis 46:2
[17] Genesis 22:1, 11
[18] 1 Samuel 3:10
[19] Acts 9:4

In each of these instances there was a major crisis in a person's life. But there was also a word from God, and we find the same here.[20]

God introduces Himself to Jacob as the sovereign of space, time and history. He rules over all:

'I am God, the God of your father. Do not be afraid to go down to Egypt, for there I will make you into a great nation.'[21]

Jacob is afraid of going out of God's will, so the Lord speaks to reassure him. We know Jacob was afraid, because that is exactly the issue which God addresses when He speaks to him. His words dispel fear and inculcate peace. God loves to speak peace to His people.

There is an additional insight in this revelation, which is the promise that it will be in Egypt that the growth to nationhood will take place.[22] Jacob is taught that God is not tied to any particular locality and that Egypt is just a step on the journey to possessing Canaan. In the broader purposes of God revealed in the Bible, Egypt is a stepping stone to possessing the world. We have a picture of the ultimate fulfilment of God's plan in the book of Revelation:

You (Christ) are worthy to take the scroll and to open its seals, because you were slain, and with your blood you purchased men for God from every tribe and language and people and nation.[23]

It is God who sends Jacob down to Egypt, and it is God who goes with them to Egypt.

---

[20] Boice, *Genesis*, 206
[21] Genesis 46:3
[22] Kidner, *Genesis*, 208
[23] Revelation 5:9-10

"I myself will go down with you to Egypt, and I will also bring you up again."[24]

That promise is very important, because for four hundred years these people were to endure hardship in Egypt. Towards the end of their time there, it was to become particularly difficult. Yet God sent them there. That is the point of this being in the Bible. Often it is in God's will that His chosen people endure suffering in this life. Why, we do not know. Perhaps it is to accentuate the glories that are to come.

This is the first time God has spoken to Jacob since Joseph's dreams. It has been many a long year since he last had a theophany, that is, an appearance of God in human form, in fact not since his encounter at Peniel on his return to Canaan from exile in Paddan Aram.[25] Now that Joseph has been found, now that the unity of his house has been restored, now that Jacob's spirit is renewed, God speaks again. He tells Jacob that it is good for him to go down to Egypt. He will go with him and will one day allow his offspring to return. God's special favour will be with him.[26]

God will not speak to anyone again until He appears to Moses in the burning bush about 430 years later.[27] The Patriarchs (Abraham, Isaac and Jacob) were prophets, that is to say, God spoke to them about His future purposes. He never spoke directly to Joseph, however, although He did speak indirectly about his future rule over his brothers through the dreams. As to God's larger purposes for His

---

[24] Genesis 46:4
[25] Genesis 32:22ff
[26] Genesis 46:3-4
[27] Exodus chapter 3

people in the future, Joseph only knew of them from the promises made to his forebears.

A chosen people

> *Then Jacob set out from Beersheba. The sons of Israel carried Jacob their father, their little ones, and their wives, in the wagons that Pharaoh had sent to carry him. They also took their livestock and their goods, which they had gained in the land of Canaan, and came into Egypt, Jacob and all his offspring with him, his sons, and his sons' sons with him, his daughters, and his sons' daughters. All his offspring he brought with him into Egypt.*[28]

There follows the names of those who went down to Egypt. Why does the Bible give us such lists of names so often? These names are in the Bible to teach us that God knows the names of every one of His children. That is why so much of the Bible is given over to personal names. These people are meant to be important to us, and they are certainly important to God. Moses tells us that in all seventy souls went down to Egypt.[29] Why is this? Seventy is a round number used elsewhere in Scripture to express the idea of totality and comprehensiveness. In other words, the whole family went down to Egypt. Not one of them was missing. This is the way it is with God's church:

> *You are a chosen people, a royal priesthood, a holy nation, a people belonging to God.*[30]

---

[28] Genesis 46:5-7

[29] The number 70 is probably arrived at by adding the names of Jacob and Joseph. The nation in miniature is represented by this ideal and complete number and is a microcosm of the nations.

[30] 1Peter 2:9

A separated people

Why did God move this family from Canaan to Egypt for the next 430 years? We have noted before that while they lived in Canaan they were in danger of losing their identity as a distinct family altogether. There was much intermarriage with the Canaanites already, and given another generation, the family bond would have been broken and forgotten. Added to this were the terrible religious practices of the Canaanites, so far removed from the standards God expected of His people. Once in Goshen, the family would be left alone to develop in an area of such lush vegetation that, once the famine was over, it would be like paradise to them. Because the Egyptians did not mix with shepherds, there would be no chance of intermarriage leading to a loss of identity. They would have time and space to develop into a new nation. I read recently of one individual in the early nineteenth century who went to America and married. The writer reckoned that by the early part of the twentieth century this one couple had over a million descendants in the US. So it shouldn't surprise us that in 430 years the descendants of Israel had grown into a group the size of a nation. No wonder that by the time of Moses the authorities in Egypt tried to stop any more Israelites being born![31]

What did the departure of Jacob and his family mean for the Canaanites? They were left to develop in their sin and rebellion against God. The restraints were withdrawn, and though they had another 450 years to repent, they did not. Instead they were shut up to the judgment that they deserved. It is a serious thing when people are exposed to

---

[31] Exodus 1:8-22

the truth of God and then reject it. They shut themselves up to judgment. Robert Candlish,[32] writing about this story, asks what effect the children of promise had while they lived in Canaan. The answer is not good. They had raped and pillaged, they had intermarried and scandalised the community. They had not acted as a godly family at all. In fact, they had been as bad a witness as you could find. Perhaps that is why it took more than 450 years before the judgment eventually fell on these people; they were given the opportunity to recover from the bad witness of God's people.

It is a fair question to ask ourselves what kind of witness we Christians are to our own culture. Do we give the impression that we are confident in what we believe? Do they see that we are serious in our commitment to the Lordship of Jesus Christ? Can they detect any difference of values between us and the general population? We who say we belong to God must ask ourselves whether we are any different from the society around us. Are we truly counter-cultural, or do we buy into the culture and ethos of the world around us? Perhaps we feel that our own nation is racing towards judgment in the form of a famine of the Word of God. If so, we need to ponder the history of God's chosen people. It was precisely because Jacob's family had not lived any differently from the Canaanites and that generations later their descendants would not distance themselves from Canaanite idolatry, that judgment and exile would eventually come upon them too. At the time of Joseph, this family's unique identity was preserved by being physically separated from the Canaanites.

---

[32] Russell Shorto, *The Island at the Centre of the World*, (London: Black Swan, 2005), 383

Now it is important to remember that this was important at this point in the economy of God until the Messiah came from this race and the royal family within it. Today we are not called to withdraw from the world, though we are called to abstain from the world's idolatries, its pursuit of pleasure, money, sex and power. We are to be in the world but not of it.

A united people

This family had not always been united. In fact their history was one of constant quarrelling and fighting. But no longer! Apart from the actual carts, which serve to assure Jacob that his sons are telling the truth, the wealth which has been showered upon them by Pharaoh and Joseph is apparently of little interest to anyone in this family. They are all united in their joy at discovering that Joseph is still alive.

There is a great lesson from this period of Israel's history for the Christian church today. Some people seem to regard the church as a kind of organisation or a club, perhaps like a gym. The mentality seems to be that we can join up for a time, then move on to a better gym or a different club when we feel the need for a change. Others seem to think they can join if they feel like it and leave at will. But the church is not a club, certainly not a health club. Actually, belonging to it may seriously damage your health! It can, in some cases limit your job prospects, or incur the wrath of your family, and its members can almost drive you mad at times! It is a *family*, and family members simply have to be accepted and loved, we have no choice in the matter. It shouldn't surprise us when the family is flawed, for the face of the church is the face of a sinner. It is the society of saved sinners who know they need a Saviour and its people are at various levels of spiritual experience and understanding. Yet Christ loves the church (we know this because He died for her) and so should we.

12

A fresh start

The international arrivals hall at Heathrow Airport is a fascinating place to be. All human life is there. Men in suits stand holding up cards with the names of clients or customers whom they have never met. These cards vary from the personal (a Christian name or a surname) to the very impersonal (the initials of a company, such as BBC, BP or GSK). Parents eagerly wait to see a child who has been abroad on holiday. Almost inevitably, there are the walking wounded, returning from their ski trip to the Alps! But there are always some sights that cannot fail to move us. It happens when someone, sometimes a whole family, comes out of the arrivals door, looking anxiously around, searching every face to find a glimpse of recognition. Off to the side there is suddenly a flurry of activity as another individual or a group move towards them. Arms are thrown around necks, kisses are rained down on cheeks, tears flow freely, and embraces seem to last forever. The onlooker can only wonder about the story behind the emotion. How many years has it been? What difficulties or illnesses have been suffered? Why the separation?

There is a reunion as intense as any you will see at an international airport in the account of Jacob's reunion with Joseph, recorded for us in Genesis chapter 46. It is all the more striking because on this occasion we know some of the grief and bitterness and sadness that have filled the years of separation. This reunion is a triumph of the grace of God over the foolishness and selfishness of a family. There was a time when this event would have been the last thing that could have been expected. But a lot has happened in those twenty-plus years since Joseph went to Egypt as a slave. The world has changed for these people, but more importantly *they* have changed. They are being *saved* from death by famine; they are being *separated* against enmeshment in the life of the Canaanites and the life of the Egyptians; and they are being *settled* in a prosperous and productive place, where they will grow to become a great nation. God has given Joseph back to Israel (that is, the family of Jacob) as their saviour, advocate and provider.

A living, exalted and expectant saviour
It is Judah, from whom Christ Himself is descended, who is sent ahead by Jacob to find out the way to Goshen.[1] Judah's story started unpromisingly as we have seen, but God has changed him, and he has risen to become the leader of the children of Israel. Judah had offered himself as a slave in place of his brother Benjamin, and that self-substitution is reminiscent of our Lord's self-substitution on behalf of His people. Now he is going ahead of the people to lead them

---

[1] Genesis 46:28

to their place of refuge, just as Jesus our Forerunner has entered heaven to lead us to our eternal place of refuge.[2]

Their saviour is ready to meet them on arrival. Joseph even prepares his own chariot:

> *Then Joseph prepared his chariot and went up to meet Israel his father in Goshen.*[3]

He gets things ready himself and he goes himself. This must have been unheard of for such an important man, but he can't wait to see his father. What emotions and thoughts must have been going through his head as he got into his chariot and raced down the roads leading to Goshen!

As we survey the scene in our imagination, we see the hurts of the past now disappear in the glad greeting, the sobs of joy and pent up-emotion. Joseph, with his power, grandeur and graciousness, makes an overwhelming impression. He was not a man to hide his emotion where it was appropriate to show it. The son Jacob had thought to be dead for twenty years now stands before him. The wrongs of the past have been righted. It is a picture which makes us think of heaven, where God promises to 'wipe away every tear from our eyes'.[4]

The text says that Joseph 'presented himself' or 'appeared' before his father:

> *He presented himself to him and fell on his neck and wept on his neck a good while.*[5]

---

[2] Hebrews 6:20
[3] Genesis 46:29
[4] Revelation 21:4
[5] Genesis 46:29

Usually this expression is used of a theophany (an appearance of God), so the use of this particular word here is no accident. Joseph's reappearance was like an appearance of God to Jacob. As believers, we have something even greater to look forward to. Stephen, as he was being stoned, had a vision of the Son of Man standing ready to receive him,[6] and one day, when we reach glory, we too will find our Saviour ready to meet us. Jesus said that He had gone to prepare a place for us and that He would come for us.[7] The word used in the Greek translation of the Old Testament (known as the Septuagint) for this Hebrew word 'appearance', is the same as that used in the New Testament of Jesus' second coming, when he comes to receive all His people into his presence forever.[8] On that day, the one whom we believe in but cannot see, will appear before us and the watching universe in all His splendour as king.

Jacob has come down to Egypt, not for the riches, comforts and security it offers, but out of love for his son Joseph. This is evident from Jacob's emotional reaction on meeting Joseph again after so many years:

'I can die at last,' Israel said to Joseph, 'Now let me die.'[9]

In every one of Jacob's speeches in the story so far, he has talked about dying. Every other time, he's been rather depressed and hopeless about the whole thing, but not now. His attitude towards death has been revolutionised. What has made the difference? Why has this man turned from viewing death with depressing morbidity? It is this:

---

[6] Acts 7:56
[7] John 14:3
[8] 2 Timothy 4:1
[9] Genesis 46:30

'I have seen your face and know that you are still alive.'[10]

His words are reminiscent of those of aged Simeon who held the baby Jesus and sang his *Nunc Dimittis*:

'Lord, now you are letting your servant depart in peace.'[11]

Like Jacob, Simeon's dearest wish had been fulfilled, in his case because he had seen the Saviour. For the Christian, the thought of death is transformed because Jesus actually did die and rise bodily to demonstrate His power and authority over death. We serve a risen Saviour, Jesus says:

'because I live, you also will live.'[12]

Joseph had been left for dead, but had gone on to claim the highest rank possible as Pharaoh's right-hand man. In this respect, Joseph points us to the Lord Jesus, who was rejected by His own people, then 'crucified, dead and buried.'[13] But then God raised him from the dead and highly exalted Him. He is now seated at the 'right hand of the majesty on high.'[14] Joseph is just one of many types of Christ found in the Old Testament, that is, people who resemble and model the character of Jesus to some degree. We have also seen glimpses of Jesus in Judah, reminding us that no one individual in Scripture can ever fully capture the multifaceted glories of our Saviour or represent all the offices (that is, the roles and activities) of our Lord.

---

[10] Genesis 46:30
[11] Luke 2:29ff
[12] John 14:19
[13] Apostles' creed
[14] Hebrews 1:3

It is as though Jacob receives Joseph back from the dead. Jacob's response on hearing the news is like that of the disciples when the women told them that Christ was alive. Like Jacob, their faith was revived, their lives were reoriented and they became pilgrims travelling to the best land imaginable. Have we reached that place in our Christian discipleship when we want heaven because Jesus is there?

A living advocate

Then Joseph said to his brothers and to his father's household:

> 'I will go up and speak to Pharaoh ...'[15]

A good advocate can speak on your behalf in a court of law. Occasionally, if you have to speak in court, he gives you the words to say. That is how Joseph acts here. He orchestrates the whole interview with Pharaoh, telling his family what he will say to Pharaoh and what they must say when they come before him. It is because of Joseph that they have entry into the presence of the king in the first place. Without him, they would get nowhere near this living god. There is an interesting parallel here with the ministry of Jesus, our great High Priest. He is described as the only Mediator between God and man; he opens the way, smooths the path and acts as guarantor for sinners approaching God.[16]

Joseph has cleverly arranged for the family to actually arrive in Goshen before they meet the Pharaoh. But will

---

[15] Genesis 46:31
[16] 1 Timothy 2:5

they be allowed to settle there? It's one of the best parts of Egypt. Ultimately only Pharaoh can decide this, and as yet Joseph doesn't have permission for them to live there. He shows great skill in the way he tells his family what to say when they meet Pharaoh. They are to be straight with Pharaoh, something Jacob's family had not been good at in the past! A lot of things were against them. Egyptians were suspicious of foreigners, especially ones from the East. There were a quite a lot of them, so they might appear to be a potential threat. Then there was the fact that they were shepherds. This was anathema to the Egyptians, who thought shepherds 'unclean'. However, this would help Pharaoh decide to keep them at a distance, so Joseph had chosen well when he brought his family to Goshen. It was close enough to the capital (close enough to keep an eye on them), but not too close. Also, by saying they were shepherds, they were letting Pharaoh know that they just wanted somewhere to live; they didn't want new careers. So they are to tell Pharaoh they are 'shepherds', a fact Joseph carefully emphasises in his own interview with Pharaoh. He also tells his brothers to ask Pharaoh directly to allow them to settle in Goshen,[17] thereby handing the king a solution to his problem of where to settle them.

So Joseph went in and told Pharaoh, 'My father and my brothers, with their flocks and herds and all that they possess, have come from the land of Canaan. They are now in the land of Goshen.'[18]

Joseph selects only five of his brothers to attend the meeting (probably the ones who will make the best impression), and they are ushered into Pharaoh's presence.

---

[17] Genesis 46:34
[18] Genesis 47:1

A king like Pharaoh, who was also regarded as a god in Egypt, would not have had cosy chats over coffee with even the greatest of servants, so this must have been an intimidating experience. No wonder the brothers needed advice as to what to say! The king asks them what they do. He has not met them before, and he doesn't know too much about Joseph's background.

> *'Your servants are shepherds, as our fathers were.'*[19]

Then they explain that they are seeking only to 'sojourn' in Egypt. This is a technical term meaning temporary residence; they do not want to become fully-fledged citizens. This was in fulfilment of the promise to Abraham:

> *Know certainly that your seed will be a sojourner in a land that does not belong to them.*[20]

Pharaoh addresses his answer to Joseph as the official in charge of the situation and gives specific instructions. It is on the basis of who Joseph is and what he has done as the saviour of Egypt that Pharaoh is acting in such kindness towards them. They can live wherever they wish, even in the fertile area of Goshen. Not only that, but if they have the capabilities required, then some of them can become superintendents of Pharaoh's cattle. The king offers them more than their hearts could ever have conceived. Because of Joseph, nearly 'boundless favour was extended to Jacob's family.'[21] The land of Goshen is referred to as the 'best part of the land' (*metab*),[22]

---

[19] Genesis 47:3
[20] Genesis 15:13
[21] Kent Hughes, *Genesis*, 532

which perhaps is a wordplay on the 'good' (*tob*) that God intended in all of these recorded events.[23]

A bountiful provider

> So Joseph settled his father and his brothers in Egypt and gave them property 'in the best part of the land, the district of Rameses, as Pharaoh directed. Joseph also provided his father and his brothers and all his father's household with food, according to the number of their children.' [24]

Joseph's wisdom results in the children of Israel dwelling safely in the land of Goshen while there is severe famine in the land of Canaan. Here their physical and spiritual needs can be met. With the best pasture-land available, the clans of Israel can settle and prosper with security and peace. Under the care of Joseph, the family find stability and unity at last. He ensures they are provided for. They have property in Egypt, given to them by one who has power to give it, which confers an inalienable right to residency and possession.

In the next section we find the Egyptians themselves losing their right to property as they give it away to Pharaoh in payment for bread.[25] The Israelites enjoy liberty and prosperity in direct proportion to the serfdom and difficulty of the Egyptians, who sell everything they have to Pharaoh, even themselves, in order to have enough to survive. I'm amazed by the fruitless discussions by some commentators about Joseph's economic and political strategy in those circumstances. The real point is that

---

[22] Genesis 47:6
[23] Genesis 50:20
[24] Genesis 47:11-12
[25] Genesis 47:13-21

Joseph rules Egypt for the benefit of the people of God, just as Christ rules in heaven for the benefit of His elect.

Strangers and pilgrims

God's people are now in the ideal location to develop into the great nation God had promised they would become. In this separated existence, they could preserve their identity as the people of God. Goshen was well away from built-up areas where they would be more likely to intermarry with Egyptians and lose their identity. Joseph is anxious to insulate his family until God's promises to the Patriarchs are fulfilled, and we know that they were to be there for over 400 years. A lot can happen in that time!

In this provision of a place of refuge, we can see a foreshadowing of the work of Christ in separating His people from those who are not His people. Their situation then was not the same as ours in the world today, however. This isolation was quite specific to their time, because in the plan of salvation, Israel had to become an identifiable people or nation if God's purposes in the world were to be fulfilled. Today, we have to be in the world while not belonging to it but, like Jacob's family in Egypt, we too are pilgrims and strangers here. We are to 'be holy', because God is holy,[26] and the ungodly, secular world is the biggest threat to our personal holiness.

Joseph asked his family to meet him in Goshen, which was fertile land right on the border of Egypt. This was ideal because it meant they could escape relatively quickly from Egypt if they needed to. This too was part of God's long-term strategy. The way out was already being planned for and was to be fulfilled at the Exodus. They were only ever

---

[26] 1 Peter 1:16

intended to be sojourners, that is, pilgrims, travellers, people with no permanent residence. It was never the intention to settle in Goshen permanently, for God had promised them something else and they held on to God's promise.

This idea of Israel holding on to the bigger promise is apparent when we glance back at the encounter between Jacob and Pharaoh. Here is Jacob, the Patriarch, the one to whom God has given the promise of becoming a great nation, meeting the lord of all Egypt, the absolute ruler of the greatest nation on earth at the time. Pharaoh is powerful, secure in himself and lord of all he surveys. Yet here is stateless, landless Jacob, who at a human level is entirely dependent upon the king, blessing him ... twice! Here is the greater blessing the lesser. Of these two men, one had nothing of this world's goods and the other had everything, but one was the inheritor of the world and the other was going to leave it for good:

> Then Joseph brought in Jacob his father and stood him before Pharaoh, and Jacob blessed Pharaoh.[27]

The Pharaohs of Egypt were obsessed with their mortality and trying to ensure their immortality; hence the Pyramids and the mummification process. For them, 110 was considered the maximum age anyone could reach, but here is Jacob, already 130 (although he was in fact to die just 17 years later, younger than the other patriarchs). Pharaoh is impressed and wants to know the secret.

Jacob doesn't exalt himself above Pharaoh, he is gracious and respectful; but nor does he refer to himself as his servant, as his sons had done. He bears witness to the

---

[27] Genesis 47:7; see also verse 10

brevity of life and the difficulties he has been through, but once again he confesses that his life has been a pilgrimage (he manages to get that in twice).

And Jacob said to Pharaoh, 'The days of the years of my sojourning are 130 years. Few and evil have been the days of the years of my life, and they have not attained to the days of the years of the life of my fathers in the days of their sojourning.' And Jacob blessed Pharaoh and went out from the presence of Pharaoh.[28]

He talks about his fathers and 'the days of their sojourning'. His identity in Egypt is that of a pilgrim. This man who has a precarious, landless existence, never doubts the promise of a more permanent land. He is on his way to the heavenly city.

Nothing gives a person a greater sense of distance from the great and powerful of this world. In the end, all the world can rob us of comes down to goods and chattels. It can take our lives, but it cannot rob us of heaven. It was this that scared the Romans when the early church was born into its Empire. Here were people who believed in a better resurrection. The world holds nothing that can entice such people. The great ones of the world do not impress such people. True believers cannot be bribed or bought. They serve a higher king, live under higher orders. Don't we want to be such people?

This is in fact Jacob's finest hour. In the next few chapters this man, who was a bit of a disaster in his younger years, is going to witness a good confession. Here is the start of it. As he stands before the great Pharaoh, he is unmoved by his greatness. How can this be? It's because he has first stood before the Lord of all the earth, the God of galaxies,

---

[28] Genesis 47:9-10

the Sovereign of history! When you have been confronted by such a God, little monarchs and chief executives and presidents take their proper place. They themselves, whether they know it or not, are clay in our God's hands, they are His servants, whose wills are bent to do our God's will. Here is this pagan king becoming the means by which God's purposes in the world are worked out. His great Empire and his civil service and his famine relief fund actually exist to serve the saints who will inherit the earth!

A lasting city

Goshen was to be their place of refuge and provision for over 400 years, but it was not the ultimate destiny God had promised. Indeed, not even Canaan was to be their ultimate homeland. As the writer to the Hebrews explains, God always had in mind another homeland. Pharaoh gave them the best of the land, but it is the destiny of God's people to inherit the world. Hebrews 11:13-16 sheds light on the way Jacob and all these people thought at the time:

> *These all died in faith, not having received the things promised, but having seen them and greeted them from afar, and having acknowledged that they were strangers and exiles on the earth. For people who speak thus make it clear that they are seeking a homeland. If they had been thinking of that land from which they had gone out, they would have had opportunity to return. But as it is, they desire a better country, that is, a heavenly one. Therefore God is not ashamed to be called their God, for he has prepared for them a city.*

This tells us that the Patriarchs' true fatherland was heavenly. But we must not identify it with heaven. Our fatherland is the new earth under the light of the new heaven. Heaven on earth is the destiny of the believing people of God.

No eye has seen nor ear heard, nor has the heart of man conceived, the things that God has prepared for those who love him.[29]

All this is ours through the work of our Champion, King Jesus, who reigns in glory. There is no salvation outside of Christ. What we owe to Him will not be made clear until that day when we stand before Him, feel the warmth of our welcome home, and enter into the joy of our Lord. What a reunion that will be! To meet and see face-to-face the Saviour we have only heard about and loved weakly and falteringly, to embrace Him and to feel His love wipe away forever all the accumulated tears of our lives – what a day that will be!

As Jacob saw Joseph roll up in his fancy chariot, as he looked round at his family united at last, he knew that everything was in place for the next stage of the outworking of God's promises to Abraham, Isaac and himself. And he looked forward to another day. Only dimly, of course... but he saw that now he could go home, really go home, to the city of God, and that one day there would be a reunion to beat all reunions.

We too have a Saviour. He is alive from the dead and lives now in the power of an endless life. We have an Advocate who represents us to the Father. I wonder if you ever think of His work for you. Do you think He pleads with God to let you off when you sin? Do you think He pleads for mercy for you? No, the New Testament tells us that God is faithful and just to forgive us our sins.[30] It says that we have an 'Advocate with the Father, Jesus Christ the Righteous'.[31] When He pleads for us, He asks for justice because He has

---

[29] 1 Corinthians 2:9
[30] 1 John 1:9
[31] 1 John 2:1

done the work that makes it right for the Father to be kind and generous towards us. It was for Joseph's sake that Pharaoh gave Israel the best of the land. It is for Jesus' sake that God gives us all things. We too have a Provider who has gone ahead to 'prepare a place for' us. Joseph's provision for Israel was not the final provision of God for His people. It pointed forward to something else, to a time when, to use Jesus' words, 'many will come and recline at table with Abraham, Isaac and Jacob in the kingdom of heaven.'[32]

Do you know these words, written by Bernard of Cluny in the twelfth century, which sum up this longing for this New Jerusalem?

Jerusalem the golden, with milk and honey blest,
Beneath thy contemplation sink heart and voice oppressed.
I know not, O I know not, what joys await us there,
What radiancy of glory, what bliss beyond compare.

They stand, those halls of Zion, all jubilant with song,
And bright with many an angel, and all the martyr throng;
The Prince is ever in them, the daylight is serene.
The pastures of the blessèd are decked in glorious sheen.

There is the throne of David, and there, from care released,
The shout of them that triumph, the song of them that feast;
And they, who with their Leader, have conquered in the fight,
Forever and forever are clad in robes of white.

O sweet and blessèd country, the home of God's elect!
O sweet and blessèd country, that eager hearts expect!
Jesus, in mercy bring us to that dear land of rest,
Who art, with God the Father, and Spirit, ever blessed.

---

[32] Matthew 8:11

13

Facing the Future

The life of Jacob spans half the book of Genesis. This is surprising when you think that for most of his life he really doesn't emerge as a particularly attractive character. By his own wiles he stole the birthright from his brother Esau to achieve that which God had promised to him in any case.[1] We have a little more sympathy for him when he is betrayed by Laban, his future father-in-law, tricked into marrying Leah and made to work fourteen years for Rachel, the girl he truly loved.[2] Later, as his family slowly disintegrates into chaos and anarchy, it's hard not to wonder how much Jacob is to blame, and in the later stages of his life, he seems to allow himself to sink into self-preoccupation and self-pity. There have been moments of trust and betrayal, sterility and fertility, feast and famine, separation and reunion, and all this within the promise and

---

[1] Genesis 25:29-34
[2] Genesis 29

providence of God. There has also been that high point where Jacob refuses to bow to Pharaoh but rather blesses him in the name of God. At that point he is taking his place as the spokesman of God and assuming his role as a vehicle of God's purposes in the world.

At the close of chapter 47, after seventeen years in Goshen, Jacob is on his deathbed. He's been talking about dying for years, especially during those depressing years after the disappearance of Joseph, his favourite son. He reminds me of the hypochondriac who was always complaining he was sick and found no sympathy from his family, who were frankly bored with his complaints. When he eventually died, he had arranged with the undertaker to have these words carved on his headstone: 'I told you I was sick'!

This time Jacob really is sick and dying, yet in a remarkable way this ranks alongside his blessing of Pharaoh as one of the greatest moments in his life. Sometimes people bear witness as much in their dying as they did in their lives. Somehow their whole life's work is focused as they lie dying and they are able to make an impact for God even on their deathbed. I rather think we should pray from time to time that we would die well. What I mean is that, when dying, we should pray that our faith would shine brightly and that we would witness a good confession to our risen Saviour.

Dying well

In these final chapters of Genesis, Joseph first brings his own two sons to his father for his blessing, and then Jacob pronounces prophetic words over all his own children. It is significant that God uses his servant Jacob to set the scene for the next phase in the life of Israel the nation. The way of the future is predicted with great care and precision. All this is done to emphasise the sovereignty of God over the lives of these people and to point us to God's saving intention to keep His promises and send one who would be both a Saviour and Ruler. Jacob knew that the people of his line, the nation Israel, would inherit Canaan, but he was also given a vision further into the future. Beyond Israel's possession of Canaan lies something greater, because the people of God will one day possess the entire world. Jesus spoke of His people inheriting the earth, while the apostle John spoke of the new heavens and earth which are the destiny of God's children, resurrected people in a renewed and restored universe.[3] Israel's possession of Canaan is but a pledge and sign of that greater reality.

This should help us to lift up our eyes to our future inheritance as God's people. In the language of Peter, 'we have an inheritance that can never perish, spoil or fade, reserved in heaven for us.'[4] These chapters are meant to strengthen our confidence that just as God was working in the lives of Jacob and his family long ago, so He is working in our lives now.

As he becomes aware that death is near, Jacob, the man of God, witnesses to his trust in God. He is living now in a pleasant place, a safe place, surrounded by the incredible luxury of Egypt, but he doesn't let that distract him. He is not moved or impressed by these things, nor does he lose his grip on the heavenly realities. It is often hard for us to think about eternity when our hands are reaching out to grasp the world. I heard only recently about an old

---

[3] Matthew 5:5; Revelation 21:1
[4] 1 Peter 1:4

friend who has made shipwreck of his life. As he became preoccupied with money, things were beginning to unravel for him spiritually and morally, although his friends had no idea this was happening. Money and security assumed an importance for him beyond anything you would have expected, especially from someone who claimed to trust in God. It can happen to any of us. When Jacob is living at last in the lap of luxury, however, such things mean the least to him. He is getting ready for heaven and does not lose sight of his reward. Interestingly, it is this part of the story that is commented on by the writer to the Hebrews.

By faith Jacob, when dying, blessed each of the sons of Joseph, bowing in worship over the head of his staff.[5]

As Jacob stands and worships leaning on his staff and asks to be buried in Canaan,[6] he is bearing witness to his faith in God's promises to him. Jacob is speaking as a believer, and as he speaks, he is God's instrument in shaping the future. He is less concerned about the unknown that lies ahead of him in death than he is about the future of God's people. It is an incredible statement of faith.

The grace of adoption

Although Joseph is governor of Egypt, he does not want to be considered an Egyptian. There is of course nothing wrong with being an Egyptian, but he wants to identify himself with the people of God and the unfolding promises of God. He is concerned about what will happen to his two sons, who were born of an Egyptian woman. Will they be lost to Israel and have no part in the promise of the covenant?

---

[5] Hebrews 11:21
[6] Genesis 47:30

After this, Joseph was told, 'Behold, your father is ill.' So he took with him his two sons, Manasseh and Ephraim.[7]

When Jacob hears that Joseph is coming, he summons all his strength. At this point Scripture gives him his 'official' name, Israel:

then Israel summoned his strength and sat up in bed.[8]

This indicates that he is about to speak and act as the bearer of the promise of God. And he does this remarkable thing.

First, he *clarifies his calling*:

Jacob said to Joseph, 'God Almighty appeared to me at Luz in the land of Canaan, and there he blessed me and said to me, "I am going to make you fruitful and will increase your numbers. I will make you a community of peoples, and I will give this land as an everlasting possession to your descendants after you."'[9]

This speech is intended to demonstrate to us Jacob's authority to confer the blessings to be outlined in these chapters. He is not acting as a private person or as your run-of-the-mill believer. He is a patriarch. He has had a personal encounter with the Living God. It is God's blessing on Jacob that empowers him to bless the twelve tribes.

Second, he *adopts Joseph's sons* as his own. This whole section is framed in legal language, because Jacob is about to perform a legal act of adoption. Here he verifies his credentials, then says, 'your two sons born to you in Egypt

[7] Genesis 48:1
[8] Genesis 48:2
[9] Genesis 48:3-4

before I came to you here will be reckoned as mine.'[10]
He calls them by name, emphasising the intentionality in
what he is doing. Certain elements of the ancient adoption
process in both the Bible and in ancient Near East practice
are evident in this section. First, the *adopter* is identified by
name, and it is Jacob's covenant name Israel that is used.
Secondly, the *adoptees* are formally identified through
interrogation of the father:

> When Israel saw Joseph's sons, he said, 'Who are these?' Joseph
> said to his father, 'They are my sons, whom God has given me
> here.' And he said, 'Bring them to me, please, that I may bless
> them.' Now the eyes of Israel were dim with age, so that he could
> not see. So Joseph brought them near him, and he kissed them and
> embraced them.[11]

Next certain physical acts reinforce the oral declaration;
Jacob puts the boys on his knee and then lays his hands on
their heads to bless them.[12] For Jacob, the sight of Joseph's
children reflects God's blessing after years of heartache.
As the adoption ceremony ends, Joseph bows down with
his face to the ground. It is his way of acknowledging that
Jacob is the vehicle of God's promises. Joseph testifies to
the gift of God in giving him the boys in the first place;
they have been such an encouragement to him after years
of affliction in Egypt.

Thirdly, Jacob *invokes God's blessing*:

> 'The God before whom my fathers Abraham and Isaac walked,
> the God who has been my shepherd all my life long to this day, the

---

[10] Genesis 48:5
[11] Genesis 48:8–10
[12] Genesis 48:10–13

> *angel who has redeemed me from all evil, bless the boys; and in them let my name be carried on, and the name of my fathers Abraham and Isaac; and let them grow into a multitude in the midst of the earth.'[13]*

The threefold pattern of the invocation here anticipates the later revelation in Scripture that God is triune: God is the God of his fathers; God is the Shepherd of his people; and God is the Redeemer of his people.

Elective grace

The elective process really begins in the adoptive ceremony. We see Joseph here carefully trying to stage-manage the whole event so that Manasseh, the older boy, gets the blessing of the right hand. But Jacob openly and gloriously crosses his hands:

> *When Joseph saw that his father laid his right hand on the head of Ephraim, it displeased him, and he took his father's hand to move it from Ephraim's head to Manasseh's head. And Joseph said to his father, 'Not this way, my father; since this one is the firstborn, put your right hand on his head.' But his father refused and said, 'I know, my son, I know. He also shall become a people, and he also shall be great. Nevertheless, his younger brother shall be greater than he, and his offspring shall become a multitude of nations.'[14]*

From before Jacob was born, he was kicking against the normal law of the firstborn,[15] and here Jacob was perpetuating the elective principle he himself had

---

[13] Genesis 48:15–16
[14] Genesis 48:17–19
[15] Genesis 25:26

experienced when he, as the younger brother, gained the blessing reserved for the firstborn from his father Isaac, as recorded in Genesis chapter 27. This is a reminder that God has His own agenda and that it doesn't necessarily follow the normal flow of expected patterns or social norms. He does things His way. Ephraim is chosen to be the leader, and so he was to become. Eventually, after the split-up of the tribes following Solomon's death, the tribe of Ephraim was to dominate the northern kingdom of Israel.

A similar theme of election runs through the rest of the blessing ceremony. Reuben is the firstborn son, as Jacob readily acknowledges:

> *'Reuben, you are my firstborn, my might, the first sign of my strength, excelling in honor, excelling in power.'*[16]

He has everything going for him from a human point of view, but his place is taken by the sons of Joseph. Jesus taught that 'the first will be last, and the last shall be first'.[17]

The greatest blessings are heaped upon Judah and upon Joseph. That is particularly significant in light of Judah's previous behaviour, particularly with regard to Tamar. Reuben, Simeon and Levi are specifically chastised for wickedness that they had committed,[18] and yet, in God's grace, blessing is pronounced upon Judah, in spite of his previous sin. God has been at work in his heart, refining him, bringing him to true repentance and a willingness to sacrifice himself for others. All the brothers had repented of their actions towards Joseph and there had been reconciliation within the family, but there were issues

---

[16] Genesis 49:3
[17] Matthew 19:30
[18] Genesis 49:4-7

from the past that disqualified Reuben from leadership. And subsequent events proved Jacob's prophecy true. The biggest change had taken place in the heart of Judah, who had recognized how unrighteous he was and had demonstrated by his actions his change of heart.

This demonstrates the principle that God's grace is displayed in God's choice. His ways are not our ways. The Bible reveals how God regularly overturned the traditions of His people by bypassing the inheritance rights of the natural heir, and here, once again, the tables are turned as Reuben and Levi are sidelined in favour of Joseph's sons, and the leadership is handed to Judah.

The doctrine of election is built into the whole fabric of the Biblical narrative, so that we learn that God is both in control and has authority to act as he pleases in His world. He also acts in accordance with the covenant promises He has made to His chosen people in the past. Here is how Paul explains election to the people of Corinth:

> *Brothers, think of what you were when you were called. Not many of you were wise by human standards; not many were influential; not many were of noble birth. But God chose the foolish things of the world to shame the wise; God chose the weak things of the world to shame the strong. He chose the lowly things of this world and the despised things – and the things that are not – to nullify the things that are, so that no one may boast before him.*[19]

Looking to the future

> *Then Jacob called his sons and said, 'Gather yourselves together, that I may tell you what shall happen to you in days to come.'*[20]

---

[19] 1 Corinthians 1:26-29
[20] Genesis 49:1

Chapter 49 records the last great prophetic statement in the book of Genesis. There have been many others, of course, but Jacob's is the last one. It acts as a summary of what has gone before and it also acts as a faith-builder for us. God is giving us a picture of the future to fuel our hope. It is important to keep in mind that this is straightforward prophecy. It is not Jacob looking at his sons' character traits and then making an educated guess about their future. No, he is speaking as a patriarch and a prophet about the long-term future of the tribes of Israel. He is speaking about what will happen in the days to come, a phrase translated as 'in the last days' elsewhere in the Old Testament.[21] In so doing, he is bearing witness to the fact that God decrees whatever comes to pass. This is a truth Christians often struggle with, I fear. Certainly there are some people who don't believe that God knows the future, far less plans it. They say He can only react to what happens. Others think He plans some things but not all things. Yet if we are to take the Bible seriously and if we are to take these chapters seriously, then we have to say that God ordains everything. Throughout the story of Joseph, God has been driving home this truth to us, that He is guiding and ordering the little events of life, the experiences of all of us, even our genetic code, to serve both our good and His glory.

As far as Reuben is concerned, the moral of the loss of his birthright is that sin has consequences. In fact, Jacob's three oldest sons all receive negative reports. By contrast, Judah is given positive promises. There is no more convincing evidence of the true conversion of Judah than the change in the way his father deals with him here. The early days of this character were not promising, but he had moved to

---

[21] Isaiah 2:2; Micah 4:1

the place of leadership through his willingness to sacrifice all for the sake of another. The change was thorough and complete. Now he is ready to take his place in the flow of history that will lead to the Messiah himself.

The first part of Judah's blessing involves his brothers 'praising' him, a play on his name, which means 'praise'. He will be praised among his family and he will put his hand 'on the neck of his enemies',[22] a way of describing authority, dominion and victory over his enemies. Jacob describes Judah as a lion, strong and powerful.[23] It is from this verse that the popular Jewish idea of the 'lion of Judah' developed. It was a common image of the coming Messiah. In the New Testament book of Revelation, John records an incident regarding the one worthy to open the book with seven seals which is held in God's hand. No one is found worthy and John weeps until one of the elders comes to him and says:

> 'Stop weeping; behold, the lion of the tribe of Judah, the Root of David, has overcome so as to open the book and its seven seals.'[24]

As the prophecy continues, Jacob becomes more specific. Judah's tribe is destined to produce kings, and this will continue until 'Shiloh comes'.[25] That is the Hebrew word and it is left untranslated in the King James Version. The NIV translates it, 'until he comes to whom it belongs.' The ESV has 'until tribute comes to him' while the Hebrew reads, 'Until Shiloh comes.' There is no consensus as to the exact translation, but a there is a unified understanding of

---

[22] Genesis 49:8
[23] Genesis 49:9
[24] Revelation 5:5
[25] Genesis 49:10

the main point. The 'kingship' signified by the 'sceptre' and 'staff' would remain with Judah until the Messiah comes. A fourth-century Jewish Targum puts it like this:

> until the Messiah comes, whose is the kingdom, and him shall the nations obey.[26]

Another ancient text from the Dead Sea interprets it to mean this:

> until the coming of the Messiah of Righteousness, the branch of David, for to him and to his seed has been given the covenant of the kingship over his people for everlasting generations.[27]

It has even been pointed out that the numerical value of the consonants of the Hebrew 'Shiloh will come' is equal to that of the Hebrew word for Messiah.[28] So in both Jewish and Christian thinking this is a Messianic promise, and this prophetic promise and blessing was to be fulfilled in King David and his house, and eventually in King Jesus. He is the Lion of the tribe of Judah, and He will reign.

What kind of reign will this be? Jacob refers in verse 11 to a donkey, which was the mode of transportation of a tribal chief throughout the Middle East. It is no surprise to learn that as Jesus rides into Jerusalem on a donkey's foal, he is welcomed by the people who see this as a kingly statement and a fulfilment of Jacob's prophecy. 'Hosanna, son of David,' they cried, meaning 'save us'.[29]

The donkey is tied to the 'vine' in Jacob's prophecy, a

---

[26] Quoted in Kent Hughes, *Genesis*, 552
[27] Quoted in Waltke, *Genesis*, 615
[28] ibid, 616
[29] Matthew 21:9

symbol of fertility, joy and peace. Grapes of the vine were a treasured produce, and to tie up your donkey to such a fruitful vine was an indication of being super-rich. In other words, one has so much it doesn't matter if the donkey helps itself! This idea of prosperity is further enhanced with the metaphor of doing your washing in wine.[30] This reign will be characterised by luxurious abundance.

There seems to be a direct allusion to this prophecy in John chapter 2, when Jesus performs his first miracle at Cana of Galilee. He turns about five thousand gallons of water into the finest wine, and when the master of the feast tastes the new wine, he calls for the bridegroom and says:

> *'Everyone brings out the choice wine first and then the cheaper wine after the guests have had too much to drink; but you have saved the best till now.'*

And John adds this comment:

> *This, the first of his miraculous signs, Jesus performed at Cana in Galilee. He thus revealed his glory, and his disciples put their faith in him.*[31]

Here was wine as plentiful as washing water, as was mentioned in Jacob's prediction, yet it was in fact water turned to wine. Did this bring Jacob's words to Judah to their minds? It may well have done, since the Messianic implications of Jacob's prophecy in relation to Judah were taken for granted by the time of Christ. It is clear that this miracle was crucial in confirming the disciples' faith in Jesus.

---

[30] Genesis 49:11
[31] John 2:10-11

But Jacob's prophecy has another dimension. Here it is again in full:

> *'The sceptre will not depart from Judah, nor the ruler's staff from between his feet, until tribute comes to him; and to him shall be the obedience of the peoples.'[32]*

The reference here to the 'peoples' or 'the nations', as it can also be translated, is very significant. Up to now in Genesis there has been a narrowing down of God's purposes. Out of all humanity, God has singled out Shem, Noah's son and the father of the Semitic peoples, and called one man, Abraham, and from him one nation, Israel. Out of Israel (God's new name for Jacob), the promise is narrowed down to one tribe, Judah and to one individual within that tribe, 'Shiloh' (however it is translated). But one day the purpose of God is to open out once more to include the world. We think of Jesus' claim and commission:

> *All authority in heaven and earth is given to me, therefore go and make disciples of all nations.[33]*

That is still happening today, as the gospel of Christ reaches out to Africa and Asia, to China and Turkey and Peru and Thailand, and the 'obedience of the nations is his.' And one day 'at the name of Jesus every knee will bow and every tongue confess that he is Lord to the glory of God the Father.'[34]

Of course, the blessings that come to all these tribes of Israel are nothing compared to the blessings in store for us

---

[32] Genesis 49:10
[33] Matthew 28:18-19
[34] Philippians 2:10-11

today because of the work of Christ. They are but a foretaste of the blessings that come upon God's church. The children of Israel inherited lands and goods; we inherit the world to come. Even now we have heavenly blessings of status and privilege which they could not have dreamed of. God the Father 'has blessed us in Christ with every spiritual blessing in the heavenly places.'[35] Matthew Henry wrote:

> *as long as we have an interest in God's covenant, a place and a name among his people, and good hopes of a share in the heavenly Canaan, we must account ourselves blessed.*[36]

The book of Genesis begins with a man living in a garden who is virtual king of creation, with dominion over every created thing. Through sin, Adam loses that kingship and that dominion. Now, at the end of the book, the promise is made more explicit that one was coming who would be king and have dominion and that his kingdom would be more lavish and more wonderful than even Eden was.

Having conferred these blessings on his sons, Jacob repeats his desire to be buried in Canaan.[37] This is his final statement of confidence that God will fulfil his promise. He even wants to be buried not with his beloved wife Rachel, but with his fathers, Abraham and Isaac. He died believing and was 'gathered to his fathers'.[38] That expression is a first hint of an afterlife. The Egyptians believed in an afterlife, which is why they embalmed the bodies of their deceased. They believed they would need a body to function in the

---

[35] Ephesians 1:3
[36] Quoted in Currid, *Genesis*, Vol.2, 387
[37] Genesis 49:29-32
[38] Genesis 49:33
[39] Ecclesiastes 3:11

afterlife. The Bible says that 'God has set eternity' in the human heart.[39]

After embalming, Jacob is given a state burial in Canaan.[40] He is honoured in death even by the Egyptians for Joseph's sake. The text records the whole company in a great procession making their way to Canaan. His burial there makes a public claim on the promises of God and on the Promised Land. Even in death, he is laying claim on the covenant-keeping God. The Israelites were concerned for proper burial rites. This was their way of indicating their belief in the resurrection. The Old Testament implies throughout that while death ends the opportunities for serving God in this life, it doesn't end the presence of God with us. Genesis has already given us a clue to the afterlife in the translation to heaven of Enoch.[41]

Amazing assurance

On their return from their father's funeral in Canaan, the brothers are filled with fear. How will Joseph deal with them now their dad is dead? Has he truly forgiven them? This problem of whether there can be true forgiveness pervades the whole of Scripture. It appears first at the beginning of Genesis, with the story of Adam and Eve, and is resolved only in the death of Christ. When Joseph's brothers see that their father is dead, they say:

> *'What if Joseph holds a grudge against us and pays us back for all the wrongs we did to him?'*[42]

They just can't believe that Joseph's forgiveness is real and permanent. Their own natures incline them to think of

---

[40] Genesis 50: 1-14
[41] Genesis 5:24, Hebrews 11:5
[42] Genesis 50:15

revenge, and they assume the same of Joseph. So they seek him out and speak to him:

> So they sent a message to Joseph, saying, 'Your father gave this command before he died, "Say to Joseph, Please forgive the transgression of your brothers and their sin, because they did evil to you." And now, please forgive the transgression of the servants of the God of your father.'[43]

'Joseph wept when they spoke to him,' and his tears and testimony serve as the climax of the story and of the book. They have nothing to fear. He has no interest in taking revenge. He knows that he is not 'in the place of God'; in fact he realizes that God has been in everything that has happened. His rejection by them, their hostility to him and their leaving him for dead, then their selling him for twenty pieces of silver, was all part of God's plan:

> Joseph said to them, 'Don't be afraid. Am I in the place of God? You intended to harm me, but God intended it for good to accomplish what is now being done, the saving of many lives. So then, don't be afraid. I will provide for you and your children.' And he reassured them and spoke kindly to them.[44]

They can be sure of forgiveness because of what God has done. Joseph does not pretend his brothers had not sinned, but recognises that God had overruled their sin.

There is no stronger statement in all Scripture of the sovereignty of God than these words of Joseph. He simply believes that God even uses the sinfulness of humans to bring about His good purposes for the world. God is described

---

[43] Genesis 50:16-17

[44] Genesis 50:19-21

[45] 1 Tim.6:15-16

throughout Scripture as the 'blessed and only Sovereign, the King of kings and Lord of lords … to him be honour and eternal dominion.'[45] In this case, God had turned their sin in rejecting Joseph around, so that it led to their salvation and, because the Messiah was to come through Judah, to salvation for the world. We need never worry that God wills everything that comes to pass. He rules the universe for the sake of His people. He guides history to the conclusion He has planned. Ultimately, Joseph's words here find their fulfilment in our Lord Jesus. He was despised and rejected by men; He came to His own and His own people did not recognize Him; He was betrayed by one of His own disciples for thirty pieces of silver. It was all so wrong. But Peter assures the people of his day that Christ was 'delivered up according to the definite plan and foreknowledge of God.' It was those people who had 'crucified and killed' him. But God had been at work even through their sin and had 'raised him up'.[46]

The end of the beginning

Genesis concludes with the death of Joseph. He has had a full life and has lived long enough to see his great-grand-children, but in the end he dies. This is the destiny of us all, unless Jesus should return. But Joseph leaves us with one last gift. He asks that his bones be preserved and buried in Canaan, the Promised Land. He predicts a mighty deliverance in the future.

> Then Joseph made the sons of Israel swear, saying, 'God will surely visit you, and you shall carry up my bones from here.'[47]

---

[46] Acts 2:23-24
[47] Genesis 50:25
[48] Hebrews 11:22

This is a reference to the Exodus:

> *By faith, Joseph, at the end of his life, made mention of the exodus of the Israelites and gave direction concerning his bones.*[48]

But it is also a reference to that even greater event which the Exodus foreshadowed, the victory of Christ. At the transfiguration this was the word used in the discussion between Moses, Elijah and Jesus when speaking of his cross-work, his 'exodus'.[49] That victory would mean life from the dead. One of the ways Old Testament believers showed that they trusted in a future resurrection was their insistence on being buried in Canaan. Hebrews 11:19 teaches that, 'Abraham reasoned that God could raise the dead.' Jesus Himself said:

> *a time is coming when all who are in their graves will hear his voice and come out – those who have done good will rise to live, and those who have done evil will rise to be condemned.*[50]

The last words of Genesis in the Hebrew are the words, 'in Egypt'. They set us up for the next part of the story. Eventually, over 400 years later, the Israelites would leave Egypt and enter the Promised Land. Much later, 'Shiloh' Himself would appear and achieve an even greater deliverance. Today we wait for this same 'Shiloh' to come again and bring about that eternal life that He has so freely promised to those who trust in Him.

To the end of his life Joseph lived as a stranger in Egypt, with his bags packed ready to go home. Even when he died

---

[49] Luke 9:31
[50] John 5:28-29

there, he had an eye to his ultimate destiny. As Christians, we too live here as strangers and pilgrims, but our focus is an empty tomb somewhere, that speaks of life.

A few more years shall roll,
A few more seasons come,
And we shall be with those that rest
Asleep within the tomb;
Then, O my Lord, prepare
My soul for that great day

O wash me in your precious blood,
And take my sins away.

Tis but a little while,
And He shall come again
Who died that we might live, Who lives
That we with Him may reign;
Then, O my Lord, prepare
My soul for that glad day.

Horatius Bonar

Bibliography of works cited

Donald Gray Barnhouse, *Genesis,*

Begg, *The Hand of God*

James Montgomery Boice, *Genesis* Volume 3

F. F. Bruce quoted in Currid, *Genesis*, Vol.2

Brueggemann, *Genesis*

John Calvin, *Genesis*, Grand Rapids: Baker Book House 1979

John Calvin, *Institutes of the Christian Religion,* trans. F. L. Battles (The Library of Christian Classics 20; Philadelphia: Westminster Press, 1960), 1.7.4.

Robert Candlish, *Studies in Genesis*

Tony Campolo, www.beliefnet.com/story/174/story_17423.html

John D. Currid, *Genesis*, (Evangelical Press)

Ruth Gledhill, Societies worse off 'when they have God on their side' in *The Times,* September 27, 2005

Kent Hughes, *Genesis*

Matt Jenson, *The Gravity of Sin: Augustine, Luther and Barth on homo incurvatus in se* (London: T&T Clark, 2007)

Derek Kidner, *Genesis*

K. A. Kitchen quoted in Waltke, *Genesis*

George Lawson, *The History of Joseph*

Lloyd-Jones, *Studies in the Sermon on the Mount,* Vol.2

Donald MacLeod, *The Person of Christ*

William Perkins, *A Commentary on Galatians*

A. Plantinga, *Not the Way it's Supposed to Be*

Richard Rice, John Sanders, Clark Pinnock and William Hasker, *The Openness of God: A Biblical Challenge to the Traditional Understanding of God*, Downers Grove Il, Inter Varsity Press

A. Leland Ryken, *How to Read the Bible as Literature*

Philip Ryken, *Galatians*

Mark Sheridan, ed., *Genesis 12-50*, Vol. 2, Ancient Christian Commentary on Scripture (Downers Grove, IL: InterVarsity Press, 2002)

Russell Shorto, *The Island at the Centre of the World*, (London: Black Swan, 2005)

Spurgeon, *Metropolitan Tabernacle Pulpit*, Volume 41

Joni Earecksen Tada, *A Step Further*

William Temple www.ccel.org/s/schaff/history/2_ch08.htm -

von Rad, *Genesis*

Waltke, *Genesis*

John Walton, *Genesis, The NIV Application Commentary*

Wenham, *Genesis*

Westminster Confession of Faith V:I (Edinburgh: Free Church of Scotland, 1955

Tell me the Story:
The Carpenter
Alex MacDonald

Alex retells these eye-witness stories of Jesus. These people tell their stories as eye witnesses of those who were actually there. They are:

> Mary, mother of Jesus, Gaius Maximus, centurion, Joanna's story of John The Baptist, woman at the well, Simon the Pharisee, Gadarene Demoniac, Jairus, Simon Peter, Rich ruler, Bartimaeus & Zacchaeus, John and Marcellus a Roman officer.

Using Biblical, contemporary and background data, Alex MacDonald skilfully tells the stories of those who were with Jesus at key points in his life.

It unfolds as if you were on the spot looking on. The stories are based on factual evidence of what really happened. This book will capture your imagination causing you to ask "What would my reaction have been if I had been there?" or "Was this really what happened"?

Alex MacDonald is the minister of Buccleuch & Greyfriars Free Church of Scotland, Edinburgh. He is married to Evelyn and they have four Children, Katharine, Douglas, Alison and Robert.

ISBN 9781845502850

Esther, A true first lady:

A post-feminist icon in a secular world
Dianne Tidball

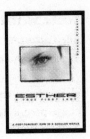

At the beginning of the 21st century women and men find themselves in a world which seems to be 'post' everything – post-Christian, post-modern, post-evangelical and even post-feminist.

How should Christians react? Is it possible to find belief in the middle of all the topsy turvy values?

The Bible tells us of a secular society in which the concept of God as we know it was unknown. Esther and Mordecai lived, loved, had faith and took courage in a godless secular empire.

We find a feminist icon, Queen Vashti, who stood up to a male dominated regime to the extent that a law had to be passed against her for fear that other women would do the same.

Esther, by comparison, is a post-feminist icon. She did not fight the patriarchal system or attempt to win rights for women. Instead she worked within a corrupt and debauched society by personal influence – never losing her vision of God or a sense of humility.

The challenge of this book is that you might prefer Vashti to Esther, the challenge of the Christian faith is that God's ways are not necessarily our ways.

Includes bible study questions to help group study in a fresh and challenging way.

ISBN 9781857926712

Bible Boot Camp:

Spiritual battles in the Bible and what they can teach you
Richard Mayhue

Today's fast-paced society beguiles us to do what you can get away with. The concept of 'moral fibre' is considered laughable, yet admired in films and yearned for in relationships. How do you develop real moral character? Richard Mayhue helps us achieve that goal by looking at character building examples in the Bible.

There are four parts to the book:

Warning: Some Failed to Win, Solomon, Jonah and Eve are among those examined.

Hope: Some Fell But Recovered While Fighting, Elijah, Habakkuk and Moses are among those examined.

Encouragement: Some Fought to Victory, Joseph, Job and Ruth are among those examined.

Wisdom: Gaining God's Perspective summarises the lessons from the previous chapters. Richard aims to teach us how to develop moral courage because true Christian education should be based on developing character.

What you are is more important than what you know when facing unforeseen circumstances.

ISBN 9781845501051

Christian Focus Publications
publishes books for all ages

Our mission statement –

STAYING FAITHFUL
In dependence upon God we seek to help make His infallible Word, the Bible, relevant. Our aim is to ensure that the Lord Jesus Christ is presented as the only hope to obtain forgiveness of sin, live a useful life and look forward to heaven with Him.

REACHING OUT
Christ's last command requires us to reach out to our world with His gospel. We seek to help fulfil that by publishing books that point people towards Jesus and help them develop a Christ-like maturity. We aim to equip all levels of readers for life, work, ministry and mission.

Books in our adult range are published in three imprints.
Christian Focus contains popular works including biographies, commentaries, basic doctrine and Christian living. Our children's books are also published in this imprint.
Mentor focuses on books written at a level suitable for Bible College and seminary students, pastors, and other serious readers. The imprint includes commentaries, doctrinal studies, examination of current issues and church history.
Christian Heritage contains classic writings from the past.

Christian Focus Publications, Ltd
Geanies House, Fearn,
Ross-shire, IV20 1TW, Scotland, United Kingdom
info@christianfocus.com

God's Hall of Fame
Peter Lewis

The Hall of Fame members in Hebrews chapter 11 are - Abel, Enoch, Noah, Abraham, Sarah, Isaac, Jacob, Joseph, Moses, Rahab, Gideon, Barak, Samson, Jephthah, Samuel and David. How can your life continue their story?

"God has heroes too! Those in the present we live with, those from the past give us examples from which we must learn. Today's heroes must learn from those of yesterday. This book provides invaluable insights as to how God views his heroes - compulsive reading!"

Clive Calver, President of World Relief Corporation, U.S.A.

"With his usual blend of spiritual scholarship and pastoral care, Peter introduces us to two lost assets in the church today: the ability to stand in awe and to walk by faith. God's Hall of Fame is packed with great theology - but you may not realise it, because it is all beautifully wrapped in telling phrases, powerful pictures, incisive application and a modern feel. Not just a good read, but a book of hope, comfort and vigorous challenge."

Brian H. Edwards, Former President F.I.E.C. and author

"When Peter Lewis comes out with a book, the church is always enriched - and this book is proof of that!"

R.T. Kendall

"This is a very satisfying book... it brings us biblical role models for healthy living... a book for one and all."

Geraint Fielder, Author and broadcaster
Former minister of Highfields Church, Cardiff

ISBN 9781857925296